Embrace Property

The key secrets to property success

Peter Iwaniszewski

Copyright 2016 Peter Iwaniszewski

ISBN: 978-1-326-60669-5

The moral rights of the author have been asserted.

All rights reserved. Apart from any fair dealing for the purposes of research or private study, or criticism or review, as permitted under the Copyright, Designs and Patents Act 1988, this publication may only be reproduced, stored or transmitted, in any form or by any means, with the prior permission in writing of the copyright owner, or in the case of the reprographic reproduction in accordance with the terms of licences issued by the Copyright Licensing Agency. Enquiries concerning reproduction outside those terms should be sent to the publisher.

Typesetting and cover design: Oxford Literary Consultancy

CONTENTS

TESTIMONIALS 7

INTRODUCTION 13

ABOUT THE AUTHOR 15

WHAT YOU WON'T GET FROM THIS BOOK 19

THE MAIN PROBLEMS AND CHALLENGES NEW INVESTORS CAN FACE AND HOW TO OVERCOME THEM 21

THE EMOTIONAL JOURNEY OF A PROPERTY INVESTOR – ADOPTING AN INVESTOR'S MIND-SET 27

CONFRONTING THE FEAR FACTOR 31

UNDERSTANDING THE PROPERTY MARKET 33

SO WHY PROPERTY AND WHY WOULD YOU INVEST? YOU NEED TO PROVIDE FOR YOUR FUTURE 37

1. STRATEGY AND PLANNING IS KEY TO YOUR SUCCESS ... 43

2. FINDING A GOLDMINE AREA IS SO IMPORTANT 51

3. THE DIFFERENT WAYS TO GENERATE PROPERTY LEADS AND FIND MOTIVATED SELLERS 55

4. DOING YOUR DUE DILIGENCE IS KEY 65

5. YOU MAKE YOUR MONEY WHEN YOU BUY 75

6. PROPERTY IS A BUSINESS AND NEEDS TO BE TREATED LIKE ONE FROM DAY ONE 89

7. DON'T LET LOW SOLD PRICES PUT YOU OFF INVESTING 93

8. YOU WILL NEED TO LEARN HOW TO SUCCESSFULLY MANAGE YOUR CASH FLOW 97

9. THE IMPORTANCE OF NOT RELYING ON ONE INCOME STREAM 105

10. PROPERTY IS A NUMBERS GAME 137

11. WHY BUILDING YOUR PROPERTY POWER TEAM IS SO IMPORTANT 145

12. SURROUND YOURSELF WITH LIKE-MINDED PEOPLE 155

13. ALWAYS ACT WITH INTEGRITY AND HONESTY AND AIM FOR A WIN/WIN SOLUTION 161

14. LEARNING FROM SOMEONE WHO HAS BEEN THERE AND DONE IT IS KEY – FIND A GOOD MENTOR 171

15. SET REALISTIC BUT CHALLENGING GOALS 177

16. EXPECT UPS AND DOWNS ALONG THE WAY 181

17. PERSISTENCE IS KEY 183

18. LEVERAGE IS KEY 187

19. IGNORE THE NOISE AND ONLY TAKE ADVICE FROM THOSE WHO ARE PROVEN IN PROPERTY 195

20. EMBRACE A CHANGING MARKET AND ALWAYS KEEP LEARNING 201

21. AIM FOR MORE THAN ONE TENANT TYPE WHEN INVESTING 207

22. INVEST FOR CASH FLOW AND RETURN –
CAPITAL GROWTH IS THE ICING ON THE CAKE 209

23. NO EMOTION 213

24. MASTER ONE STRATEGY BEFORE MOVING ON 217

25. DELAYED GRATIFICATION 221

26. BELIEVE AND HAVE FAITH IN YOURSELF 225

27. PAYING YOUR ENTRANCE FEE 227

28. NEGOTIATION 231

MISTAKES TO AVOID LIKE THE PLAGUE 248

SO WHAT CAN YOU DO NOW? 254

BONUS CHAPTER: WHAT WOULD I DO IF I WAS
STARTING OUT AGAIN TODAY? 256

A BIG THANK YOU 263

TESTIMONIALS

Peter has an encyclopaedic knowledge of property investment and regularly shares his knowledge and experience with other property investors. I am pleased that he has written this book so that even more people can benefit from his guidance on how to invest both wisely and profitably. In my view it is a must read for every property investor.

Nigel Reynolds

Chartered Certified Accountant, Reynolds and Co

www.reynoldsandco.co.uk

Peter is one of life's great guys. Peter is a true example of what hard work and focus can achieve. I have been fortunate to work alongside Peter for many years and have picked up great knowledge of the property market from the book which has helped me considerably in my day to day role and personal arrangements. I cannot recommend Peter's service's highly enough. A true example of learn before you earn.

Ben Clay, Wealth Manager,

True Potential Wealth Management.

Peter is so grounded and knowledgeable and sincere and this shows through in this book. The day we started the mentorship with Peter really started us on our property journey and within 6 months we were buying cash-flowing properties. We have gone from strength to strength with Pete's help and advice.

Phil and Lorraine Thompson

A very informative, educational book which gives the theory and the practicality of how to be successful in property. I have now been working with Peter at Embrace for 8 months and found my first two rent to rent properties that cash flow £1,200 per month. Peter supported me to set them up and manage them. I would say to anyone in property you need support if you want to make a success out of property.

Chris Pagett,

www.cppropertieslettings.co.uk

Pete was one of the first people I met in property many years ago and we began our own property networking event shortly after in the West Midlands. We have continued to work closely together over the years. Pete is the real deal – he continues to be a very active investor as well as spending his time helping others reach success. A truly genuine and knowledgeable guy who is a great friend and colleague.

Jackie Goodman
Property Investor, Consultant & Mentor
Host of Black Country PIN & Shropshire Property Meet

A fantastic book for people looking to be successful in property. Peter's journey is both informative and inspiring.

Stewart Warden

Mortgage broker, Principal of Claywarden Associates

www.claywarden.co.uk

Peter has walked the walk in property investment and this shows through in the book through his practical and honest approach. A must read if you are looking for the key fundamentals needed for property success.

Steve Friel

Managing Director Central Electrics

www.centralelectrics.com

Disclaimer:

I have taken care to make the figures and specifics in this book as accurate and relevant as possible at the time of writing; and of course I hope you understand that these can change depending on market and economic forces.

The content, projections, figures and indications contained here in this book are based on opinion and cannot be relied upon when making investment decisions. As with any investment, property value can fall as well as rise.

The author offers this information as a guide only and it cannot be considered as financial advice in any way. Please refer to your independent financial advisor who is qualified to give you complete advice based on your circumstances.

The author Peter Iwaniszewski is not qualified to give mortgage, legal or financial advice. Please seek legal and financial advice from a qualified advisor before making commitments. Neither the author nor 'Embrace Property Ltd' accept liability for decisions made based on the contents of this book.

This book is a guide only.

INTRODUCTION

You have probably found and picked up this book because you are looking to understand more about property investment and how you too can use property to become financially free. This may not be the first book about property that you have read. You may have already found and read other books which have promised the earth but failed to deliver what you want: clear, concise and easy-to-follow content which I trust you will get from this book.

The reason this book is different is because it has come from years of 'on-the-ground' experience, making some mistakes which I learnt from and fine-tuning my craft. I was once where you were all those years ago, wanting to learn more about property investment and not knowing if all the hype that surrounded it was indeed just that - 'hype'. I was fortunate to deal with some very inspirational individuals who guided me in the right direction and I thank them all as they allowed me to change my life and become financially free. I would like to help you now in the same way as they helped me. It makes such a difference having this help because it can seem very confusing and overwhelming without it, so I hope I can do the same for you too.

I have been fortunate enough to build a multi-million pound property portfolio and I don't say this in any way to brag or boast. I say this because I was just a normal guy in my twenties with a dream, ambition, and a strong will to succeed. I have had hurdles to overcome and many challenges to face (anyone who tells you it is easy is lying or hasn't walked the walk!) but I came through. I started investing in supposedly one of the worst times in history at the start of 2008 so if I can do this, you can do this now too. In this time I have learnt some key fundamentals which guided me through, and these can be used in a rising or declining market. I share them with you in this book.

You may already be doing very well in another field, and you can transfer those skills over to property investment. Being successful in property is no different to any other business - it takes time, effort and commitment to following proven processes. The saying 'success leaves a trail' is certainly true and from the very fact that you are reading this book you are already going against the grain and not listening to the 'naysayers', so I congratulate you for that.

Let's face it, we live in a very tough world. One of the great parts of life is the amount of choices we have and opportunities that are out there. The downside is that because of this it also means there are many different strategies out there which can be confusing and overwhelming, so it can be hard to find out which is best for you and who you can trust. Integrity and honesty are very important to me so this book is based not only around different strategies and key points to consider, but also the truth and reality of day to day investing as opposed to the ideal of how you might like it to be.

ABOUT THE AUTHOR

If you're anything like I was seven years ago, you're understandably a little wary or cynical of a stranger making big claims to you about property investment. It's absolutely right that you should be. It's essential that you always do your due diligence and make an informed decision rather than trusting anyone and everyone. I'm including a little about myself by way of a short introduction so that you can get to know me before you continue, but there is more about me on the back of the book for you to read.

To begin with I have to say I believe I am just a normal man who had a dream to one day run my own business (well I suppose not that normal with a surname like mine! It has certainly been memorable with estate agents over the years!)

But seriously, I am just an average man who found a passion in property and business and followed this dream. I truly believe that if I can do it, then so can you. I will cover more about reasons for doing property and identifying your reason 'why' later in the book, but I will share a few of my main reasons for wanting to be successful. If we're honest, most of us like the finer things in life: nice cars, big houses, and luxury holidays, amongst other things. Whilst these are nice, I found myself with a bigger reason for wanting to succeed. Ever since I was little my mum has unfortunately had MS which for those who do not know is short for Multiple sclerosis, a nervous system disease. Now ever since I can remember my Mum had been going to a specialist hospital in Cambridge to get information on her disease and what was currently being done to make progress. I can still picture it now, driving down there to see my mum when she stayed for a few days, and having to listen to my dad's Abba CDs which were his favourite at the time (that's enough about my dad's dodgy music tastes, although I have to confess I don't mind a few of the songs myself!). Now I vividly remember that there was not a cure in sight unfortunately, but I also know that if it does come in the future then it likely will not be cheap.

My mum suffering this disease gave me a strong will to succeed to hopefully one day pay for the cure, or if none is available, then at least make her life as comfortable as possible. It has been said before that if what you want has enough emotion attached, then you will overcome any barrier to get this. We will all have reasons like this that are so compelling it motivates us to go that extra mile, and you will need to know yours to follow your dream and block out any negative opinions you get (there is more on this later).

Moving on, I am not a DIY expert or tradesmen which many people believe you need to be to succeed in property. I didn't have a property background as such and up until 2008 I followed a traditionally 'normal' route. I went to university in 2003 and graduated in 2006, and after spending that summer having fun and trying to avoid getting a Job, I finally got my first Job in recruitment in 2007. That was a really good experience and I will always be thankful to that particular company for seeing something in me and giving me a chance, particularly as I didn't have any experience. As an employer myself today, I strive to do the same and I always look at the person and their enthusiasm and attitude, not necessarily just the experience they have. It was only after getting made redundant in 2008 that I began to think about Job security and exploring my own business as a route as well.

I remember at this time feeling very nervous and unsure about my situation and life in general. I had just brought my first residential property in 2007 right at the top of the market. I managed to get £3000 off the asking price which at the time I was over the moon with as it was my first experience of negotiating on a property!

Shortly after I bought it, the UK experienced one of the biggest recessions in history and any money I had negotiated off quickly disappeared! This was certainly an unexpected introduction into property as you can imagine for a new investor starting out. To say I was not concerned would be a lie, however I also saw a massive opportunity moving forward and always remembered many entrepreneurs I had read about saying they had made their highest profits in a recession. I quickly learned the importance of buying high cash-flowing assets that would be able to survive a market downturn if needed (something very important which we will cover later in the book).

I am naturally a cautious person but before I embarked on my property journey back in 2008, I read extensively around the subject and became convinced that property was the safest way to secure my future. This really inspired me and I began to research property as a business and made it my goal in 2008 to meet and talk to as many people as I could who were already successfully investing in property.

As I said earlier, at the time I was working in a job in recruitment that I didn't particularly like and every day used to walk over to the shops nearby to buy my lunch. If I could see myself now I dread to think what I looked like walking back for another afternoon in a job I really didn't like (I'm sure many of you may be able to relate to that feeling, although I sincerely hope you can't!) It was at this point I managed to see a property seminar advertised in my local Tesco which was based at the Hilton Hotel one evening. I had arranged a game of tennis that evening but decided to cancel as something told me that this was an opportunity to find out more.

This led me to my first property seminar in 2008 and from there I never looked back. To this day I remember walking in and feeling like I had entered another world. There I was in a room full of other people looking to find out how they could become financially free. It suddenly appeared real and whilst still very nervous, I felt an extreme sense of excitement.

I also felt uncertain and isolated when I decided to leave my full-time job in 2009. I was told by many of my colleagues that I must be mad to leave it in such uncertain economic times. Although I was fearful, I still followed my path in to property and business. I told myself that I had to make it work, and made a decision that's what I was going to do.

WHAT YOU WON'T GET FROM THIS BOOK

You won't get hype from this book or lots of 'get-rich quick' information. If you are looking for a 'get-rich quick scheme' whereby you can be drinking champagne on a beach for very little effort, then this book is not for you. By all means, have that as an end goal, but it does take effort and time to get there. The good news though is that if you are looking for proven techniques that can change your financial life by building an asset base, then please keep reading.

Simple and easy

This section is very important to me as it allows me to 'get real' with you straight away. I think you will definitely appreciate me giving you the reality, and it will make you much more prepared in the long term. Property is not easy and there will be difficulties like in any other line of business. There will be things you have to do that you don't have the answer to yet, that you don't understand, and you will have to go through challenges, but once you do and you learn what to do, then things will become easier. It is just like walking or riding a bike that is easy for most of us now but wasn't always easy when we first tried!

People saying property is easy baffles me. Straight after university when I got my first job in recruitment I had to learn about the role, educate myself, get trained and continue to learn every day. Property is no different, it requires effort, dedication, and education but the results can be endless. Property investment is like everything else and the principles are relatively simple, but there is a difference between 'simple' and it being 'easy'. If something is simple then someone can give you the blueprint and their experience and a list of things to do, and if you follow those blueprints and secrets and stick to them, you should get where you want to go. As mentioned, they can also give you some warnings to make sure you try and avoid the mistakes others have made in the past. By following this blueprint you can use it to take you from start to finish like a roadmap, and you should achieve the success that the person who has given you the blueprint has (that's why it is so important to model successful people which is discussed further in this book). This is how you start and then you can move on from here and this is what wealthy people do to always keep learning and bettering themselves. How wealthy you want to become and what level you want to take it to is down to your own personal goal.

You will have to understand however that property investment is not easy (as everyone would do it) but it is simple when you follow proven blueprints and concepts.

The sky is the limit but we have to start at the start, and learn the fundamentals. These will be your solid foundations long term.

THE MAIN PROBLEMS AND CHALLENGES NEW INVESTORS CAN FACE AND HOW TO OVERCOME THEM

We have been in one of the biggest recessions in history since 2008 which has also brought with it huge opportunities and profits for those who find the courage and are willing to go against the grain.

Whilst there is great opportunity, this also means that property investors are now facing new challenges every day associated with this huge opportunity. The good news is that by identifying these challenges it means that you can take positive strides towards eliminating them, meaning they should not block you're investing journey. Here are some of the main challenges you're likely to experience:

Changing markets and regulations

The property market is always changing and you can make money in any market providing you know how. When I started my journey at the end of 2007 the market was already changing. The credit crunch had started to take effect, and property prices were coming down. There was a tightening up on mortgage criteria meaning many people were finding it hard to get finance. At the time of writing this book in 2015 the market has been showing signs of recovery, and it will change again I'm sure over the coming years. It is important to realise this and always keep up to date with changing regulations and the changes in the market. You can do this by surrounding yourself with the right people and a team of experts who can keep you updated, and this is something we will talk about more later on.

Overwhelm/confusion

Sometimes no sooner does an investing opportunity become real, it becomes confusing and overwhelming. There is just simply so much information out there. There is so much free, but often conflicting, 'expertise' on forums and social media sites. As a new investor it's difficult to know who you can trust and which strategy to start out with. There are many advanced strategies that people beginning try to start with. In my opinion, it's always best to start out with the basics and learn the core fundamentals which is what this book is about. Whichever strategy you do choose I would urge you to choose one, or maybe two at the most, so you can avoid becoming overwhelmed and confused, as this can halt your progress.

Lack of focus and clarity

This is something I have seen first-hand with many people in the past and finding focus was definitely something I needed to do myself when I began investing. There can be many distractions that will keep you from following the path that you originally set out on and you must control the urge to keep changing your focus. This is something I had to learn to do myself at the start, and it is became very apparent that I needed a strategy and plan to keep me focused and clear on my goals. The saying 'follow one course until successful' is certainly true and this is what allowed me to avoid being distracted by other opportunities. That is not to say that you will not expand into other areas, however to avoid getting distracted and wandering, it is vitally important to achieve your first goal before moving onto something else.

Lack of finance

This is one of the biggest barriers with people looking to invest in property as most people are conditioned to believe that you need to have lots of money to invest in property. However if these particular individuals dug a bit deeper they would realise that there are different strategies in property that do not require lots of start-up capital and therefore they could still profit if they knew how to.

Lack of time

We are all busy and most people in life feel that they don't have enough time to do everything they would like to. Property investing is often one of the things that people think about or want to do, however they feel they don't have the time to do so. The irony of this is that if you invest extra time now to build your property portfolio, you will become financially independent in the future, which means that you can retire early and spend all of your time then doing whatever you want to do, as you will not need to work for a living. You may have heard the saying that 'you need to work hard enough so that you don't have to'. We all have the same amount of time in a day or year. It's a matter of deciding how you spend or invest your time, so we need to use it well.

Lack of knowledge

There are many people who really want to invest in property but have no idea of how or where to start. When I first started I was the same and after using 'trial and error' I also knew that I had to get myself educated and learn my craft. Investing in knowledge and investing in yourself is key and one of the best investments you will ever make. A lot of people are not prepared to invest in their property education and this is one of the reasons they will not gain the knowledge they need.

The fear factor

It is an emotionally challenging time when embarking on any new venture and property investing is certainly no different. There is a 'fear factor' for anyone starting out and it is important to remember that this is a totally natural feeling. We have all heard the horror stories with property investing from people who have lost money in property, to others who have had nightmare tenants. It is true, there can be problems associated with property investing just like any other business or walk of life, but in reality most problems can be mitigated. It is only natural to feel fear but you often find the people who let fear paralyse them into a state of indecision, end up spreading that fear to others. They are not sure what to do or see it as such a risk that they do nothing, and because of this try to put others off investing in property too. I have found fear to be a very good motivator in the past and healthy nerves are in my opinion a good thing. For example, we all hear of people who have had nasty food poisoning but we don't stop eating food. Or we have heard of drivers having nasty crashes, but we don't stop driving cars. Instead, we take precautions to protect ourselves.

Fear only becomes a major problem when it stops you from taking action and realising your dreams. I have seen this happen many times in the past to people and it is a real shame, as they do not realise how close they are to life changing results. It is something I feel is a very important hurdle to overcome, which you can do so it does not affect you on your journey.

THE EMOTIONAL JOURNEY OF A PROPERTY INVESTOR – ADOPTING AN INVESTOR'S MIND-SET

I sometimes feel that this topic can get overlooked so I consider it vitally important to outline it in the book. I feel it is a more important factor than most people think, and it is by adopting the right mind-set that individuals can then make strides forward with the practical side of investing. There is no doubt that going into property investment is a big step for many people. When you learn anything new it takes time to adapt to it and condition yourself. Mind-set is talked about a lot in property and business and for a very good reason, as it is extremely important.

To be successful in property or business you need to adopt a 'rich' mind-set. This is something you can learn to do and it will help you make that initial leap of faith. Without taking the leap of faith, it means that you will not be able to move forward and start the exciting financial journey that can lie ahead of you.

It has been said before that there are different aspects of wealth which is firstly the psychology of wealth, then planning your wealth, then creating your wealth, then keeping and sharing your wealth. This clearly shows the importance of firstly adopting the right mind-set and mastering the psychological part of wealth, before moving on to the other parts. It is important to think big and not restrict yourself by thinking you cannot achieve your desired results. Napoleon Hills book ' Think and grow rich' is a very good example and I would recommend this to anyone as it shows the importance of thinking big, and this is what having an investors mind-set is all about.

Perception vs reality

There is this subject of perception and reality which I find very interesting. This is because the perception is often not the reality. The way people perceive the property world is very important as it effects the mind-set they have. If people perceive that property is dangerous and always focus on the downsides then this will become their reality, and they will have a negative mind-set. Someone with a rich mind set does not let this happen to them and does not focus on the negative perceptions that may be portrayed by others. They focus on the positives and learn from other people being successful, therefore their perception is positive which allows them to adopt the right mind set, which in turn will change their reality for the better. This is known as 'The law of attraction' which states that by focusing on positive or negative thoughts a person brings positive or negative experiences into their life.

Knowing Your "Why"

Knowing your reason 'Why' you are investing in property is a very important part of the strategy process and the one you'll come back to most often to keep you on track if you are ever tempted to quit. People with an investor's mind-set always have a strong reason 'why'.

> Important note: Your "why" is the calm undercurrent that carries you steadily forward when you feel like you're drowning in waves of self-doubt and worry.

Your "Why" needs to be so compelling that it gets you through the tough times. As I mentioned earlier my why was certainly compelling enough, and everyone's is personal to them but must be equalling compelling. It could be a job that you hate and want to leave, or it could be that you are trying to build a better life for your family and children. Whatever it is it needs to be so strong that you feel it deep within, and nothing is going to stop you from achieving your dream. You need to embrace the fact that there will be hard times and times when you will have to work long hours - we have all been there. At the end of the day though, what will keep you going is the knowledge that you are constantly moving forward towards your end goal.

It is also very important to be specific in your 'why', for example:

- What is it about this job that makes you want to leave?
- Would a shift in your focus, role or responsibilities improve the situation?
- If you got an entirely new job in a different company, would you still want to leave?

- How do you want to provide a better life for your family, is it the money or the time you crave?

Being specific is vital as it will map your route, and you are far more likely to achieve goals that are specific, and more likely to keep going if times get hard. Sometimes people like the idea of property or another business because they see it as an ideal, or are intrigued by being their own boss and owning their own business. This may not be enough when times get hard or you have to work long hours. This is why asking yourself the questions above is vital, as then you will know that you really want to leave your current role, and that coupled with a strong enough 'Why' will mean that the sky really is the limit.

Summary: Adopting an investor's mind set is key as people that succeed all have this. They are not afraid to think big and put no limit on their goals. Their why is so compelling and strong it gets them through tough times and means that they can break through any barriers that they need to.

CONFRONTING THE FEAR FACTOR

So you've decided to seriously look at property investment to help you achieve your long-term goals but, you feel yourself gripped by terror at the prospect of investing in property. I often hear many people talk about certainty - that they would do it if they had more of a guarantee. This is the time to confront your fears. At least that way you can decide whether they are rational and do something about educating yourself to overcome them, or make a fully informed decision to keep away from bricks and mortar investments. For some people buying your own home isn't as big a deal as buying a house as an investment – I guess the belief is that because you'd be paying rent anyway, it makes more sense to be putting your money into an investment, rather than simply paying off someone else's mortgage with your rent money.

Many people also make the initial step to overcome their fear of getting started but then get gripped by the 'fear of competition', which can often be a myth. A lot of people will give up based on this fear, but the fact is that many people 'trying' property investment are not really competition as they often do not know what they are doing. Owner-occupiers are not investors, and speculative investors are not either. It is only professional investors who are making property work and making real money, and they make up a small percentage of the market.

We all start somewhere and wherever you are right now is

fine so just start from where you are. By reading this book you are one step ahead than most, and are making positive strides forward. Don't let perceived competition stop you, as most people are not making as much money as they may say, and it is only professionals who are. Your job is to become one of those professionals, and you can start by overcoming this fear factor to then make your first steps into serious property investment.

UNDERSTANDING THE PROPERTY MARKET

The property market as a whole

House prices and the housing market are both a British national obsession and a key driver of the UK's consumer economy. Therefore understanding the property market is important and something which many people spend their time researching. At the time of writing this book in 2015, and since the huge crash we experienced in 2008, there have been signs of recovery and house prices have started to increase in many areas of the UK. This has prompted many more people to enter the market and look at property now they feel the market is on the rise.

I thought I would include this chapter about the property market as it is very important to understand what has happened previously, and what is likely to happen moving forward so that anyone who reads this will realise that now is a great time to buy residential property in the UK. In 2008 many people thought that this was the worst time to buy, and that now is a better time to buy as the market is improving. The reality is that from 2008 to 2015 was a great time to buy property, and from 2015 onwards is also a great time providing you know how. The market is always changing and if you change and adapt as the professional investors do, and follow some key fundamentals that you will learn in this book, then you will profit hugely.

The property cycles

The UK property is cyclical just like every other market. It goes up and it goes down. In the long term the trend in the UK has been that it goes up, due to a variety of reasons. We live in a popular country with limited space and an increasing population. A lot of the countryside is green belt and protected from development, but demand for accommodation continues to increase year after year. This is due to a number of factors including easier immigration, increasing divorce and changing social factors such as more people going to university. If you add to this the fact that the number of new homes being built has slowed dramatically due to the downturn in the market in 2008, you can see how the demand increases but the supply is limited.

The fluctuation in house prices is due to changes in this supply and demand. A simple definition of this is the amount of something available and the desire of buyers for it, considered as a factor for regulating its price. Therefore with less stock but more potential buyers, the price increases.

So we know what makes them rise but when do they rise again?

The truth is that that no one can accurately predict when a market will bottom out and start to rise again. Many people will have opinions on what they think will happen in the future, but no one can actually know. With a downturn in the market there will actually come a point where prices have fallen to such a level that it is actually cheaper for people to buy and pay a mortgage than it is to rent. When this happens people will begin to buy again and fuel a rise, as long as they can raise the deposit and get a mortgage. This has started to happen now with first time buyers taking advantage of the help to buy scheme which was a government scheme brought in to help them raise the deposit for their new homes.

Many people think that it is better to buy when the market is on the up however the people that are going to make the most money are the people who can buy at a cheap price and wait for them to go up. This concept is the same as trading in this respect.

Whatever market we are in there are always opportunities, and with prices historically rising over time, it is always a good idea to buy well and then appreciate the growth over time. This can happen with other commodities but in my opinion property is the strongest one, with the majority of the world's millionaires and billionaires making most of their wealth from property, as stated in the Times rich lists when they are published.

SO WHY PROPERTY AND WHY WOULD YOU INVEST? YOU NEED TO PROVIDE FOR YOUR FUTURE

It's a sad fact and not very encouraging that many reports often suggest that many people will struggle in retirement. As a nation we are all living longer, and that means we need more money to support us into our old age. In my opinion it is unlikely that the government will be able to support us all the way we would like. Most people can't rely on their company pension scheme or savings. Unfortunately what this means is that unless you do something about it now, you will either have to keep working beyond the normal retirement age or accept a lower standard of living in your old age. The good news is that this book will give you the insight into how you can do this for yourself, taking your future in your own hands and making it secure.

So why don't we spend all our money on cars, clothes, holidays and expensive toys like many other people? You only live once hey!

Unfortunately what most of us don't want to hear is that if you do too much of this it is a sure-fire way to end up getting yourself in so much spiralling debt that you may never escape it, and it can be paralysing.

Investing is the **only** route to financial and 'time freedom'.

Without investing in assets you will always be exchanging time for money. Without investing, your income will be directly related to your hourly rate. You will always be tied to working, and never get a residual return on those hours you work. You will only earn more by working more and there are a limited number of hours in the day even if you wanted to work every hour God sends.

The key is to not trade time for money. The fantastic thing about investing is that after the work is done once, you still keep earning from the time and effort you have put in, and so the return is endless.

I learnt that Rich people do not trade time for money, and the good news is that I also learnt that I had the choice to take the other route which was to invest in property.

There are many reasons why property is such a good vehicle and many reasons why investing in property is the right choice to make. Property statistically doubles in value every 7-10 years which I consider, in itself is enough reason to invest. Now at the time of writing this book we have been through one of the biggest recessions this country has ever seen, so it is fair to say that this may not be the case over this particular time (2008-2015), however as a general rule over the longer term this is thought to be the case. As well as capital growth, I believe there are many other reasons to invest in property both from a financial and ethically rewarding point of view.

When I first thought about property I was wrongly under the impression that this was the only way to profit from property, by waiting for this capital growth. How wrong I was. I thought it could only be a pension fund and whilst this is still true, I never thought about 'cash flow' and 'return'. It all began to make sense as I got educated in property and I realised that all successful property investors and business people focused on cash flow and return as this was the life blood of any business, and the capital growth was the icing on the cake. The truth often is that when you get the capital growth you will then look to spend this on more cash-flowing assets, or another business or property strategy that allows you to profit even more.

You may have seen Dragons' Den on the television, the programme focused on successful angel investors who invest in businesses looking for a financial input. I always liken property investing to this scenario: imagine someone going into Dragons' Den and saying to one of the dragons: "I have this great business idea. It won't make you any money on a monthly or yearly basis, but it may be worth something in ten years' time." I think, with respect, they would probably last a minute before being asked to leave the building. 'Cash flow is King' and the importance of this I cannot stress enough.

Property compounds over time as values rise, debt reduces, cash flow increases and compounding increases the capital that churns out the income.

Property in my experience is virtually passive income and about as passive as it can get. Anyone who tells you that it is completely passive is lying or trying to sell you something. It is important at all times to be honest and upfront and I would never say it requires no work at all. It does require work either managing the properties yourself, or keeping up to date with the agent who does this for you. When it is up and running though, I have found it to be one of the most passive forms of income and this can allow you to enjoy your time doing the things you want to do.

This is vitally important, and to many people I have met it is as much as, if not more of a driver, than the financial gain. How sad it is that most people spend their whole life working to earn the time and money to do the things they want to do, but then may never get much of that time as it comes too late in life. To free up your time to do the things you love you will need residual income from assets, and this is what many successful investors have done before and what you can do now as well.

Moving on, property investing has also been a very rewarding experience for me, and also many of my clients. As well as the financial gains and the free time property can provide you, it is also a great chance to give something back as well.

We have been able to house many homeless people through the local council and charities that we have worked with. This has been rewarding to us as we have seen people rebuild their lives and become independent again through the accommodation we have provided for them. This has ranged from elderly people, to single mothers looking to relocate and move forward in their lives. We also helped a couple who unfortunately found themselves needing urgent accommodation when their business went bankrupt. All these situations are very rewarding to me. I am fortunate and blessed to be where I am today, and to help people along my journey as well is very important to me.

So that's why I do property – and hopefully by now you can see the benefits of property and investing for a secure future. As mentioned earlier, this book is about giving solid information based on real experiences so that you can get not just the theory, but the reality as well. I want this book to be a good use of your time, as I realise how valuable it is to you. We cannot get time back and how we use it will dictate our results, so it's important we use it well. I would urge you to read this book all the way through, and more than once if you can, as you will get far more from it and you will see it from a different perspective each time. I often read the same book, or listen to the same audio regularly, as you can get different 'light bulb moments' each time.

So without further ado let's get on with the key fundamentals needed for property success.

1. STRATEGY AND PLANNING IS KEY TO YOUR SUCCESS

If you were to approach a bank for a business loan to start up your new business, they would certainly want to see a business plan. It should be no different with your property investing. However in my time I have seen many people start out in property who have not considered what strategy is best for them. This can be very dangerous as there are lots of different options, strategies, and ways of making money from property. Not all of these will fit you and your criteria, and so you really need to think about your investment goals and targets. This will depend on a variety of factors including your financial situation and the money you have available to invest, your risk profile, and your experience level, amongst other things.

You need to first and foremost have a vision. You will need to make that vision strong and compelling and stick to it. The key at the start is to devise a property business plan, so that you can plan where you want to be, and can also highlight any aspects, you will need to overcome or need help with along the way. From my experience you should be looking to devise at least three different plans which are:

- A 12-month pan
- A 3-year plan
- A 5-year plan

Writing these 3 plans which should outline your investment

goals and targets, will be a good exercise and allow you to get focus and clarity on where you want to be, ultimately helping you get to your end goal. As Tony Robbins said, 'clarity is power' which is very true.

It is important though to write challenging yet realistic plans. Everything usually takes twice as long as you plan. You need to set challenging goals but be realistic about how long it will take, how much it will cost, and allow/factor at least double the time/cost. There is absolutely no point in writing a plan that is unrealistic and unachievable, as all this will do is leave you frustrated and overwhelmed. The key is to not only think of what you want to achieve, but also think of potential pitfalls you may face along the way. This will allow you to plan ahead and to put provisions in place to combat potential problems. Whether that is problems with finance, growth, or mind-set issues, it will help you to focus and gain clarity on your journey. The saying, 'if you fail to plan, you plan to fail' is extremely true and all successful entrepreneurs and property investors have gone through this exercise.

When I started out I made a 12 month plan which included the amount of properties I wanted to buy that year, and what tools I felt I would need to work on to get there. The 12 month plan was all about defining my area, and building a solid foundation with agents that would benefit me for many years to come. Therefore I asked myself questions such as:

1. How many properties do I want to purchase in an ideal world?

2. What is my ideal income needed from investing?
3. What is the initial strategy I need to work on most?
4. How to I plan to generate leads initially?
5. Do I currently have money to invest or will I have to look at using strategies that do not require as much capital input to make cash flow? (There is more on these strategies further on in the book)

Doing this will give you a good idea at the start on which way you want to progress, and planning well will allow you to make better progress.

You can then move onto to make a 3 year plan which aims to take your business that step further. Therefore it may include all the things in the first plan, but also you may want to be looking at things such as refinancing your properties and releasing capital to further invest. My 3 year plan involved working on obtaining the amount of cash flow I needed to go full-time in property and then researching other strategies after this.

You can then cover points such as:

1. Do I plan to refinance properties or leave the equity in?
2. Would I like to set up a property business as well as investments?
3. Do I like the idea of training others?
4. Will I need to attract Joint venture finance?
5. When will I go part-time or full-time into property and

what income will I need?

6. Is finding a day to day business partner with complementary skill sets important to me?

Full time or part time?

At this point you may be thinking about whether you want to go full time into property. This was the time when I was beginning to think about this myself. I had been investing for a year and it was in my plans to go full time into property, and so I did begin to make plans for this.

Often I hear people say that they can't make money from property if they are not doing it full time. You obviously have to be realistic on your goals with the time you have (set realistic but challenging goals), however even if you are investing on the side or are part time there can be certain advantages to this, such as being able to get mortgages easier. Even if you are not looking to do property full time, then as long as your strategy and plan is centred on this, you can still make positive strides forward with your investing.

A five year plan and beyond is essentially then your ultimate goals for your business.

This may include looking at your ultimate cash flow goal and what aspects you want to focus on with your property business. It may focus on your end goal and what you feel you will need in place to achieve this goal. For example if you aim to have 30 properties in five years, do you think that you will need staff and what will you want these members of your team to do. You can ask yourself questions such as:

- How hands on with my property management do I want to be?
- Do I want to make management and lettings a big part of my business?
- Will I need premises and if so where would I like these to be?
- What location/s do I want my properties and business to be?
- What is the most important currency to me, time and freedom or money?
- What is my end goal in terms of income?

You can then aim to work back from this 5 year plan as well and work on what you need to achieve to get there. Some people may say that thinking this far ahead is not necessary. I believe however that you should be planning this far ahead, and a lot of successful businesses and business people do this and have this foresight. It also keeps you focused on what is important to you and what will change your life. I have often seen people follow a path they feel is right as it works for someone else but this is not always a wise thing to do. For example, someone I knew believed that buying as many properties as they could was their goal as they knew somebody who had over two hundred properties and seemed to be making endless pots of money. What they forgot was the amount of time this person put in, and the level of responsibility they had. The person I knew began buying and buying and then realised further down the line that the amount of time they had free was not enough. I believe (and from their own admission they would tell you) that they did not plan fully at the start, and did not think about the staff they would need, and the responsibility they would have, by buying so many properties. They did very well to get there, but then realised that they got into property for time freedom and a certain amount of income which they could have achieved with far less property and responsibility. Therein lies a lesson which is that it is so important to think about what you want, and what your ideal end goal is, and then you can aim to achieve this knowing that every day, and every hour you work, is getting you closer to life changing results.

> Important note: This is all about planning and goal setting which is vital. In Brian Tracey's book 'Goals' he covers the importance of goal setting, and says that you are far more likely to achieve your desired income if you have put down specific goals and dates you want to achieve these by.

Another key point to remember as things evolve is that your property investment plans may change slightly and the key is to be always thinking of ways you can tweak or improve what you are doing. Once you get used to writing and structuring different plans to suit your circumstances and investment goals, you will then be able to look further down the line at what you expect to be doing in five years' time and so on. It is vital to always be looking into the future, but also focusing on the present and how to constantly move your property investing forward.

It was something that I learned to do at the start and I also learned that to have plans changing was not a big problem as long as I was prepared and understood that I was doing this to evolve. Successful businesses and individuals do evolve and move forwards over time, and by having a clear strategy and end goal, this means you can adapt as and when you need to.

Summary: Planning is key and this cannot be stressed enough. Having set plans and timescales will get you to your goals quicker, and allow you to review your progress regularly. Always remember that plans can change due to personal circumstances and market changes, but by planning ahead you will be able to look at pre-empting any potential market changes, and make sure that you have other options in place as a back-up. For example, keeping up to date with the economy and what is going on at a government and council level is key as this will allow you to foresee any changes that may be specific to your chosen area.

2. FINDING A GOLDMINE AREA IS SO IMPORTANT

There is a lot of work to be done from when you first decide to invest in property to when you buy your first investment, and this can seem very daunting to begin with. Even if you are not actively managing your properties you should still decide on the right property investment area before you begin making any purchases.

Finding a Gold Mine area for your portfolio is one of the most important factors of your investment. By not having the right area it can affect the profitability and success of your properties massively, which is why research is key from the start.

I am a true believer that all things start from here and that only once you have found the right area will all the different strategies in property work. Over the years, I have met a lot of successful investors and there has often been one thing that has linked them all together. The common trend seems to be that they have built profitable portfolios in one, maybe two areas. This is not to say I have not met people who have invested successfully in lots of different areas, but on the whole the majority have focused their efforts on a particular area, usually fairly close to them. Ideally when looking for your own 'goldmine' area, you should be looking for an area that is no more than fifteen to twenty miles away from where you live, or no more than an hour's drive, preferably no more than forty five minutes. This is for a variety of reasons but one of the main reasons is that it is easier to manage, benefiting you both financially and time wise.

It is key to spend quality time building a network of agents, tradesmen and property professionals who will form a solid part of your team. This will then allow you to get to know the area well, meaning you will get to know the true value of properties, and also which are the best 'goldmine' areas within your chosen areas.

A lot of investors are looking for a promising area to invest, which will suit their individual strategy. It is important to note here that promising does not mean the most expensive or cheapest area. Promising means a place where people would like to live and this can be for a variety of reasons, and is essentially down to the strategy you have chosen, and the tenant type you are aiming at.

You should be asking yourself many things when looking into a potential area including:

- Where in your town has a special appeal?
- If you are in a commuter belt, where has good transport?
- Where are the good schools for young families?
- Where does my target market want to live?
- Is there a strong rental demand for my target market?

Asking yourself these questions might sound over simplistic, but they are one of the most important aspects of a successful buy-to-let investment purchase or career. By defining your exact area you will have clarity and will ask yourself the questions that are relevant to what you are personally aiming at. There are also 'areas within areas' meaning that you may find an area or city to invest, but only part of it will work for your target market, and there are certain roads which are better than others.

> Important tip: A goldmine area is an area right for you not somebody else. Take your time finding the area that suits your criteria.

Defining your property investment area is hugely important, as over the years I have seen many people look at a strategy or area that works for someone else and try and replicate it exactly. Whilst this is achievable if it is right for you, I have also seen other people get frustrated that it has not worked for them as well, but it simply could be that the tools they have available would fit a different area or strategy. This could be for many reasons including location, time available, and your financial position. It is important at the start to work out what area is right for you primarily, which will stop you looking elsewhere and using a 'scattergun' approach. When you have found an area that you think is promising you will then be able to look at the financial side of the potential properties and whether the figures stack up. We will cover how to calculate figures in another section.

As mentioned earlier I suggest that the area is within 15-20 miles of where you live if possible, as this will make it easier to build a trusted relationship with tradesmen, agents and other members of your power team. You can initially go onto to Rightmove and search this radius from where you live. This will give you an initial insight into property values and allow you to do some online research on potential yields, cash flow and returns that are available. (There is more on how to calculate yields and cash flow in another section)

Summary: Finding a Goldmine area is key for any investor to be successful in property. Your Goldmine area will be the source of profitable properties for you to buy. Once you have defined your property strategy then you will be able to focus on finding the right Goldmine area for you.

3. THE DIFFERENT WAYS TO GENERATE PROPERTY LEADS AND FIND MOTIVATED SELLERS

Most people who are selling a property will likely want to achieve the highest price, which is obvious. The truth is that maybe only every five or ten people out of every hundred will be motivated enough to give you the kind of discount you want. This is also dependant on the market conditions as well. As a property investor, you will have to become good at finding motivated sellers, and there are motivated sellers everywhere, all you have to do is find them.

There are many ways to find good property deals that suit your criteria, and this section highlights some of the main ways this can be done, both by working with estate agents and advertising privately as well.

Buying through estate agents

You would think that estate agents would be an excellent source of motivated sellers. After all, the estate agents will know when a sale has fallen through, or if the seller needs to sell in a particular hurry. This is all good in theory, but I often hear investors complain that they cannot get any good deals from estate agents because the estate agent has a shortlist of investors who they call first whenever they get a really good deal. Generally this is true and often many people don't bother to look for motivated sellers at estate agents because they think the agents will give all the best deals to their friends.

Estate agents want to sell property as quickly and efficiently as they can. If they have a good deal that they can sell by calling one person rather than having to show twenty or thirty people around the property, then they would much prefer to do that. Some of the best deals I have completed on have come from estate agents. I have sometimes been told about properties that are for sale before the For Sale board goes up, and even before there are any details produced for the property. If one of the local agents with whom I work finds a property which suits my criteria, they will often call me first, because they know if it is right, I will buy it. It saves them a lot of time and hassle, and it gives the seller the fast solution they may need to their problem.

As a new investor when working with an agent your goal should be to get on to the estate agent's shortlist so that you are one of the people they call whenever they get a good deal. Most amateur investors will walk straight into an estate agent and declare that they are looking for great below market value investments, at least 25% below market value. The estate agent will usually then roll their eyes, think 'here is another one', and explain to the investor that they are the twentieth person to come into the office that week asking for such deals. It is no surprise that potential investors who do this struggle to get good deals from estate agents.

You need to understand how to speak to estate agents in such a way that they want to do business with you on a regular basis.

You need to demonstrate to the estate agent that:

- You know what you're doing without sounding arrogant
- You are a serious investor
- You have money ready to invest
- You can act promptly, efficiently and professionally

You will also need to create mind space with the agents. This is very important in the negotiation process and something that you should aim for when building a new relationships. It is vitally important to be remembered for the right reasons so that you are at the forefront of their mind when an opportunity becomes available. You can do this in a variety of ways and we all have things that make us memorable. For me it was my surname but it could also be:

1. The type of clothes you wear
2. The fact you go in at the same time each week
3. The fact you take in cakes regularly

...amongst many other things.

All of these things will keep you in the forefront of the agent's mind which is very important in the negotiation process.

It can take time to build a trusting relationship with agents, but if you put the ground work in at the start then you will get the results for years to come. There is a section later in the book on negotiation and how to work more with estate agents.

Private advertising to generate leads

The newspaper advert strategy

Advertising in the newspaper is one way to generate leads privately. If you pick up a copy of your local free newspaper and look in the property section, you will always find adverts from buyers who are offering to purchase property for cash with a fast completion. Depending on where you live, there may be lots of buyers advertising in this way. The reason they are advertising there is because it works. If it didn't work, they wouldn't be advertising, week in, week out. Some of the buyers advertising are national companies but many of them will be local investors just like you and me.

Some investors I work with often feel it is not worth advertising in newspapers because of all the competition. I will acknowledge that yes, there may be lots of buyers advertising in your local newspaper, but I would also bet that at least half of them don't really know what they are doing, or are not full time investors. A lot of people will see someone else using a certain strategy and try to copy it, without really understanding it. I have called many buyers advertising in newspapers, just to check out the competition. I was shocked at how amateur most of the people are who answer the phone are, and how bad they are at asking the right questions. So yes, there are other investors advertising but that should not put you off, as long as you understand what you are doing. Some of the initial questions I ask when I speak to a private seller are:

1. What is the general condition of the property?
2. Is it central heated and double glazed?
3. What is your remaining mortgage amount?
4. Are there any other secured loans on the property?
5. What timescale would you like to sell the property in?
6. Is the property on the market with an estate agent?
7. Do you have a price in mind that you would like to achieve?

These allow me to get more information and a better idea of the situation which in turn allows me to think about what strategy may help the vendor before even visiting the property. You will need to run your newspaper adverts over several months. Don't expect to place the advert just once and get an amazing response. If you get a call from a motivated seller who has seen your advert in the newspaper, there is a good chance they would have called some of the others advertisers as well. You need to be really good at building rapport on the telephone, and move very quickly to take advantage of the deal, otherwise your competition will likely beat you to it.

I do not recommend you put an advert in with your local free newspaper; the response rate will fall dramatically as a lot of people put these newspapers straight in the bin.

The postcards strategy

This is an incredibly easy, cost-effective method of finding motivated sellers. However, many people overlook this method because it almost seems too simple. Investors don't believe that it would work, but it does. The basic idea is you create a small advert which you can place in the window of your local corner shops or newsagents for a minimal cost each week. It is 50p a week in my local newsagent. The copy on the postcard adverts would be very similar to that of a newspaper advert or leaflet. It just happens to be the same advert on show in one location for months and months on end. This method may not generate a lot of leads for you, but it does work as long as you have enough postcards in different shops. Don't be surprised if you don't get any response from the two postcards you have displayed, as that is not enough. Ideally you want hundreds of postcards all over the areas in which you invest. Then you need to do this regularly to really see the benefit. Even if it only brings you a few deals a year then it should more than cover the advertising costs ten-fold.

I know some investors who use this strategy very successfully indeed.

The leaflet strategy

The beauty with this strategy is that you can target specific areas in which you would like to buy below market value properties. A newspaper advert will go out to multiple areas whereas with leaflets you can narrow it down to specific roads and houses if you want to. You will need to design a leaflet which explains the service you offer and have this delivered to at least 15,000 to 20,000 households in your target area regularly. To achieve good results, you do need to deliver high numbers of leaflets, but another benefit of this strategy is that you are going direct to the seller and thus may have less competition than if they were to respond to an advert in a newspaper.

This strategy will require some capital input to pay for printing and distribution of your leaflets plus it does take some time and effort to coordinate. But the results can be well worth the time and effort required.

Many people often ask me if they should drop the leaflets themselves. I personally believe that it is not a good use of your time to distribute these leaflets yourself. You can recruit your own team of leaflet distributors. Running your own team does take some effort and you need to put checks in place to ensure people are doing what they are supposed to do, and your leaflets are being delivered, but it is often a better use of your time.

Buying leads from other investors strategy

If you don't want to set up your own lead-generating systems, you may decide that the easier route for you to find motivated sellers is buying leads from other investors. I have found some fantastic investment opportunities which have come from other investors, and I even bought one myself when I first started out in property. There will be a fee to pay for these properties so you will need to check that they work for you, and are worth the extra money.

There are two main ways of finding leads from other investors.

Firstly there is Online: There are several websites which specialise in attracting motivated sellers, and then selling the leads on to other BMV investors. This can be a very quick and easy way to find deals. However, you need to be prepared to work through a number of leads which may not be suitable until you find a good deal. You also have to be quick as there may be many other investors using this route to find leads.

Networking

This is a fantastic way to buy leads as you can get to know the other investors selling, and can build trusting working relationships. There will be many people at networking events who source deals and sell them on, and so your goal would be to find someone working in the area you want to invest, and who you can trust. You will still want to do full due diligence on the deals they offer you, so building your knowledge of the area is still key.

A dedicated website

Another way that people attract motivated sellers now is through the internet. However, on the internet you will face a lot of competition from other investors, some of whom will be spending lots of money on advertising. If a motivated seller completes an application form on your website, you can bet that they have filled in applications on a number of other websites as well, so be prepared.

> Important note: Often it is the investor who contacts the seller first who will secure the deal, as long as that investor knows what they are doing. Speed, knowledge, and being ethical and likeable are critical here.

Summary: There are many ways to find properties that suit your criteria and many people use multiple strategies for this. Remember that some of these ways will cost you and so it is important to work out what your budget is. Whatever that budget is aim to advertise regularly as consistency is key. Therefore if you only have enough money to use one strategy regularly then this can often be better than using a scattergun approach.

4. DOING YOUR DUE DILIGENCE IS KEY

So you have found a potential area that appeals to you and you have found that there seems to be a healthy supply of your target tenants, and properties available within your price range. It is now time to do your financial due diligence on each property you look at.

Due diligence is extremely important when looking at profitability of a property investment. You will need to constantly refer back to your strategy when doing your due diligence on a property purchase. It is important to remember that a property deal is only suitable if it fits your strategy and circumstances, and often no two circumstances are the same.

So what is due diligence?

The dictionary definition of due diligence is, "the care that a reasonable person exercises to avoid harm to other persons or their property." In plain English, it is simply doing your homework. Before putting your funds to work, you should get good at this. It is extremely important to remember that due diligence should be done at the start as afterwards is too late. Unfortunately in my time in property I have seen many people try to take shortcuts when doing their due diligence. Financially, this is like driving without your seatbelt on, and I would certainly warn against taking any shortcuts here.

So what does due diligence involve and what should you be looking for?

Due diligence means a number of things including taking caution with your investment, performing calculations, reviewing documents, procuring insurance, walking the streets of the potential property, amongst many other things. It is essentially doing your homework for the property BEFORE you actually make the purchase. If there are too many issues with the property and that means too much potential risk and cost, then you can cancel your purchase and look for a better property.

Due diligence is something I have done with all of my past purchases and will be something I do with all future purchases or business decisions. In my opinion it is one of the things that separates an amateur investor from a professional investor. It is also vital for minimising risk and increasing the long-term profitability of a property investment. If we do our due diligence correctly, we can minimise our risk, and our investments can stand the test of time.

One of the main things to consider when doing your due diligence is also interest rate rises, and it is something that new investors often forget. At the time of writing this book rates have been at an all-time low so it is very important at the moment to do this. This is because a property can look very appealing on a low rate, however you need to be prepared for a rise when it happens.

So what can be done to minimise this risk?

Rules when doing your due diligence

It is vitally important to have very strict rules when buying investment property, and these rules will be then be the focus when doing your due diligence to make sure the potential investment fits your criteria.

> Important Note: I said here what suits *your* criteria, and not what someone else thinks is good or works for them, as they may be following a completely different strategy and path to you.

A generic, basic set of rules for someone when they start out may be:

- Buying any property under £100,000
- Buying properties in your goldmine area
- Properties with a minimum of 15 to 20% discount
- Properties with a minimum gross yield of 8%
- 2 and 3-bed houses
- No new build or off plan properties
- No structural problems or heavy refurbishments

Now that would be a good set of rules to start, and most people who buy a property do not have a set of rules that are to that level of detail, but these for an experienced investor are very basic. They are far more things to consider than the list above (which is for illustrative purposes only) and we will be covering these in more detail now.

Ultimately your set of rules is your bible and will allow you to buy multiple properties knowing that you are following a strict criteria that works for you, devoid of emotion, and totally focused towards making a profit.

You can look at the financial side of the investments in different ways.

Firstly there is yield. So what is yield?

Yield is calculated as follows:

> Annual rent/divided by the purchase price

Yield is a way that many investors look at stress testing their investments, and yields can vary from area to area. As a generic rule in my area I aim for a yield of 8-10 %. This is widely thought of as a good rental yield for a single let property. If I am looking at a multi-let investment then I am looking at achieving a rental yield well into double figures.

Next there is cash flow. What is cash flow?

Cash flow is calculated as follows:

> The monthly rent minus all of the monthly outgoings which includes mortgage payments, insurances, management charges, and service charges amongst others

Cash flow is a very important part of any investment and you will hear me talk about this a lot more throughout the book. It is important to calculate your cash flow properly and not cut any corners here. I have seen people in the past try to exaggerate the cash flow from a property to make it look more attractive, especially if they are trying to sell the property on to someone else. This is a big mistake and I would urge strongly against this when looking at any kind of investment that presents itself. You want to be as conservative with the figures as you can to stress test the investment fully. I even take a 10% incidental fund out of the rent amount as a buffer in case of an emergency. You do not have to do this but I personally find that this acts as a good back up in case maintenance work needs doing unexpectedly.

Then there is Return on Investment (ROI). So what is ROI?

Return on investment is calculated as the annual cash-flow/total capital outlaid.

For example one of my clients is making £300 cash flow per month from a particular property so £3600 a year, and they have outlaid £25000 to buy it, which gives them a 14% ROI. I'm sure you will agree that this is a great return, and see why many people feel property is a good idea and better than leaving savings in the bank.

These are three main ways of calculating the investment potential of a property, in addition to the discount that you get as well. You can also be looking at making sure the property still cash-flows well if you re-mortgage the property, and also that you have multiple exits which is very important.

In my early days in property I was guilty of just focusing on one or two things and not building a comprehensive list of rules. What resulted was the first couple of properties I bought not being as good a deal as the hundreds I subsequently went on to buy for myself and other clients. Luckily I came out unscathed as they still 'washed their face', but I learnt that I needed to follow a strict criteria when doing my due diligence.

I remember years ago when I first started I came into contact with someone who had not focused on a strict set of rules and found themselves losing a lot of money which was not nice to see. They bought a bungalow at £200,000 which they believed after a £20,000 refurbishment would resell for at least £275,000 maybe more, giving an expected profit in the region of £50000 before tax. Not a bad few month's work I'm sure you will agree. However that was only on the surface and they had focused entirely on the discount they believed they had got. The problem they found themselves with was that, although they had achieved a good discount, they were unable to sell the property which was the strategy they had proposed to use, and unfortunately the only strategy they had considered. The property had a low yield and the rental return was not there. They were unable to sell the property at the price they wanted, and had used bridging finance to buy the property. All the costs began to mount up and they ended up losing money on this investment.

Because they were unable to sell the property and only had one exit strategy it was a very risky game to play. We will now be moving onto exit strategies and the importance of this.

Know your exit strategy when doing due diligence

Now you may be thinking that to sit down and think about an exit strategy before you have even started investing is a bit strange. It was a new concept to me when I started but I realised the importance of this after finding out that other successful property investors and entrepreneurs always did this. It is very important for a number of different reasons including the fact that it helps you minimise your risk by having more than one exit strategy available, and this section will highlight all of the reasons for this.

After thinking about it more, it made sense to me. For example, before you even walk into any bar you should know where the fire escape is. If the proverbial hits the fan and chairs and tables start flying, how are you going to get out unscathed?

So what are you in property investment for?

Knowing what you are going into property investment for should be the starting point when thinking about your exit strategy. Are you in property to leave a legacy for your children or are you primarily investing to create a business for yourself, or make enough money to pay your children's university fees. Asking yourself these questions at the start will allow you to plan your exit and it will mean that members of your team can work with you to achieve this goal. For example your accountant will understand what your exit strategy is and so should be able to present you with the most tax efficient way of achieving this.

Business and wealth can throw many things at us, and before we make any investment, business or career decision, we should look carefully at how we can get out and liquidate efficiently and cost effectively when we need too.

If you are buying property, you should know exactly when, where and how you can sell it if needed, and at what percentage under market value you will have to sell it at. You will want to know all the costs of buying and selling assets. You will want to know lead times, as the costs can mount up very quickly. Don't forget your contingencies when looking at your exit strategy.

For example if you are doing a refurbishment and it takes 9 months, what will all of those extra mortgage payments mean to your cash flow?

If you are taking out a lease on a property have you checked all the small print before you sign and are you and your solicitor happy with the contract? All these things are very important for due diligence but also when knowing your exit strategy. The last thing you want is to be tied into a 50-year lease for a property that you only want to have for five or ten years. Never sign anything unless you absolutely know what you are signing, and know how you can exit safely and cost-effectively.

You will also want to look at your tax strategy as well as part of your due diligence. I would always suggest consulting a qualified tax specialist who can guide and advise you on the best way for you to structure your business, both now, and later down the line.

This all comes down to due diligence, planning and foresight. If you use this in all your investment decisions then I am sure you are on your way to becoming very successful. Sometimes knowing when to get out can be as important as knowing when to get in, and this is crucial to remember.

Have more than one exit strategy

Whilst planning and knowing your exit strategy is very important, it is also vital that you have more than one exit strategy available. This allows you to minimise your risk even further and make sure you have covered as many bases as possible. I personally like to have at least two exit strategies available but preferably more. For example, you may be buying to let and planning to hold your property for the long term. If you do need to raise more capital for any reason at some point, what is your plan?

Are you going to re-mortgage or sell and will the property allow you to do so? If you cannot re-mortgage or sell at any given time, what is your plan then? You need to stress test your investments to make sure that there are multiple exits at any given time. This is very important and something I do with my investments regularly.

Summary: Doing your due diligence on any form of investment is key. You need to do your due diligence before you buy as after is too late. You will need to work out the cash-flow, yield and return on investment amongst other things, to ensure that the investment fits your chosen criteria and expectations. If you are looking at a potential property and haven't done so already then you should work out the yield, cash flow, and return on investment upfront. This will be a great start to see if the property works on paper. If the property stacks up financially and you feel the area is right and rents well, then you are making great strides into finding profitable properties.

Exit strategies are also of paramount importance when investing in property. All successful investors have clear exit strategies and often have more than one. This will safeguard your investment, and mean that you are in control should anything untoward occur.

Once you have planned your strategy and know what you are in property for, there are strict rules to follow when making sound investments. This section is all about what to do to make sure you buy solid investments that are profitable over time.

5. YOU MAKE YOUR MONEY WHEN YOU BUY

Although it is very important to buy for cash flow and to treat your property as a business, you also can make your money the day that you buy. You want to be looking to achieve a significant discount from the value of the property if you can. This does not always mean a discount from the estate agent's pricing as sometimes properties are priced to sell. This means a discount from what the property is truly worth. There are various online tools you can use to help guide you on this, such as websites like Right Move and Zoopla. However speaking to local agents is another way that will allow you to understand your local market, and what properties are currently selling for.

Doing your due diligence on a property is extremely important as mentioned in the previous chapter. You need to be looking at a variety of things such as previous sales, using your local knowledge, and speaking to estate agents who you know and trust. Getting a feel for market value when doing your due diligence is important. When investors begin to buy properties and invest they are looking to buy below market value (BMV). This is because they are trying to buy the property at a discount, so that they lock in equity from day one which will minimise their risk long term.

A mistake that some investors can make, particularly new or inexperienced, is that they mistake buying below market value (BMV) for buying below asking price (BAP). The assumption of many people, of course, is that asking price equates to value. This is not always true. We cannot assume that the asking price reflects the true market value as this can be dangerous. Chances are that you will not know who has set an asking price, or how they came up with that figure. The asking price might be too high, or it could be too low, or it could be just right. As you become more experienced and get to know more agents within your area, you will begin to see patterns in how they price properties, and whether on average they tend to price too high or too low. Proper due diligence will give you a feel for how close to the true market value (MV) the property is, but do not ever assume anything. This is another reason why working and focusing in one area is so useful, as it allows you to get to know an area back to front, which in turn will give you a better chance of working out the true market value of a property.

Saying that, the market value can be hard to quantify and it is not always straightforward. This is a topic that I cover regularly with my students and mentees. For example, there may not be any recent sales on a property that you are interested in purchasing. In this case you can speak to local agents to see if they are selling properties in that area and if there have been any recent sales which are not registered online yet. If not, what do they think they would sell a property there for if they were to list it? As you get to know agents well you will gain an understanding of which opinions you can trust and which provide a true reflection of market value. If you do use agents to provide an estimated market value on a property, it is advisable to ask at least three agents to get comparable views.

Different valuations of the same asset

You can also often get different valuations of the same asset and will need to contend with this as well. For example let's say you have a property that you want to sell. Do you think that your view of what the property is worth will be the same as what the person buying the property thinks it is worth? The answer is likely to be no as you have bias and emotional attachment, and are going to want to sell it for as much as possible, as we all would. You actually in all can have four different valuations of the same asset as you can have an agent's valuation, a surveyor's valuation (often as low as possible to protect their personal liability), your valuation, and also what the vendor feels their property is worth. If there are multiple agents then it can be five or six different valuations. Therefore there can be some confusion on what it is worth as it is all about perception and what someone is willing to pay.

I always feel that a property's value comes down to three things which are: what else is for sale, what's under offer and what's completed in the last three months. As a professional investor we want facts not opinions, and I am always looking at the individual market that I am investing in as my barometer. You can get asking prices and sold prices of properties from Right Move, however, as explained later on, sold prices are only one component when looking at predominately investor owned areas. The market is transient and over a three to six month period your figures might not be 100% accurate. Over a longer period you can get accurate figures on what a property is worth, based on other comparable properties. The good thing about existing property, for example '60s ex-council houses, or long rows of terraced houses, is that they're all virtually the same. There are streets with the same properties, design and layout that mean when one goes for £100k, another one is often worth in this region. Even if there is a major difference inside it's probably only going to make a small difference in the price. This is how I understand real value, but again I do not just rely on sold prices as there can be some that are low and other anomalies because they are being purchased by investors and not homeowners (More on this later).

Make money when you buy by adding value

This is another way that I have benefited from buying property, and many of my clients and business partners have as well. Now I have always had a rule with adding value that I look to make at least £2 to £3 for every pound that I spend. I have added value to properties in the past in a variety of ways and the majority have not needed major alterations, just sometimes changes in layout and additional stud walls.

The key with every transaction is adding value based on your strict criteria as mentioned earlier, but also looking at what the market you are operating in would accommodate and how you can profit from this. I remember buying a property a couple of years ago and viewing it with the agent who I knew well, and because of this they gave me their own opinion. "It's a hole Pete! were their exact words - very diplomatic I know! However, I knew by knowing my market that it was located well and, as with every property I am interested in, I went to view it to draw my own conclusion.

When I arrived at the property I could see that it looked distressed even from the outside, and I could clearly see that that it needed modernisation inside. On the other hand I could also see huge potential based on the layout and some alterations that could be made. I also saw the potential to add considerable value to the property once the refurbishment had been done. The property was on the market for 80k and I managed to secure it for 70k which on the face of it would have looked like I had got just over a 10% discount, which whilst not to be sniffed at certainly in today's market, was not the largest discount I was getting at the time. I knew though that by doing the refurbishment which came in at 7k I was able to increase the value to £100000 and so I actually created a further discount through the refurbishment. This is very important to remember.

Over-valued properties

This subject fascinates me and amazes me as well. It's all about psychology because the asking price is not always the right price as discussed before. Sometimes the vendor want to try an over-inflated price, or sometimes it can be the agent pricing high to get the listing. If they do not get interest over a period of time, then they will slowly reduce the asking price. This is something I learnt from agents over the years, whereby if they thought the price was high I would mention that it seemed quite high without offending them, and they sometimes would say that the ' vendor wants to try a higher price before they will take an offer.' It is therefore something that I will ask an agent if I think the price seems high, especially if I know them well. I will say something such as: 'is this the price your agency has listed or is it the vendor's price instruction?' This gives the agent the chance to say whether they think it is a silly price or not. This has happened in the past with certain properties that I have bought. I have asked this question and the agent has said that it is the price the vendor wants to try initially. I have been able to tell in some cases that the agent knows the vendor will accept a much lower figure if there is no interest. This has been particularly apparent on properties that need heavy refurbishment. Because of this I never take these prices as gospel and I always look for what my leverage can be, whether that be the state of the property or the fact that I can complete very quickly for example. Either way I often ignore the price and come to my own conclusion on what the property is worth to me, and then make the offer. If it is not enough then I move on. Simple.

Under-valued properties

Similarly there are also under-valued properties and again the asking price is not always the right price. During my time in property I have bought many properties which are close to asking price. This has been for a variety of different reasons. Sometimes the property is just listed at the wrong price which I never seem to understand. On the other hand the property can sometimes be priced to sell on the basis that the vendor would be prepared to sell at a discount to achieve a fast, efficient sale.

Two of the main ways I see this happen in my area are:

1. Distressed properties (repossessions)

What is a repossessed property?

A repossessed property is a home that has been seized by a lender after the previous owner defaulted on the mortgage or other finance arrangement.

Once a lender has taken ownership of a property, they will seek to sell it quickly in order to recoup the money that has been loaned to the previous owner.

So why are repossessed properties cheaper?

This all comes down to the way lenders approach these sales. They are legally obliged to seek the 'best possible price' in order to serve the interests of the previous owner, but they often do not do much to prepare the property for sale.

Lenders often want to sell repossessed properties quickly, so will usually price them below the market rate and offer them for sale immediately. As a result, repossessed properties often sell for up to 30% less than might be expected through a private sale.

Therefore they are priced very competitively and below the actual value that they may achieve on the open market. If you can act fast either with cash or a mortgage that is approved then you have an opportunity to pick up some very good deals.

I remember a property that came to the market that was a repossession and I got a phone call from the estate agent. Now I knew the agent fairly well and I think they thought I was going to offer what they thought was a silly price. The property came to the market at £59950 and it was going to generate a fair bit of interest at that price. I went to view the property straight away and saw that the property needed a few thousand spending on it to get it to the rentable standard required. I offered £57k which was what the agent said would be enough to agree the sale and I think the agent was shocked, as they thought I may ask them to try a lower price. So why would I offer so close to the asking price, surely as an investor I would want the largest discount possible?

Well that it is a very good question and one I am asked regularly. It all comes down to the value not always be the asking price and knowing your area well. I knew that the property was actually worth in the region of £75k and so it was still a bargain at £57k and I would have paid asking price if needed. I knew this from the extensive research and due diligence I had done, (as mentioned earlier due diligence is key) but also because I had a similar property valued recently in the area, which is another advantage of working and knowing your area very well, and buying in the same types of areas.

I was able to exchange quickly on the property which is key with repossessions as it has to be advertised up until exchange, and I had secured a property I was very happy with and still have today. This point is very important as I often see many people make the mistake of equating asking price to value. Therefore they would have looked at the property and thought they will offer 20% below as this is their rules and they would have likely not got anywhere and been told it was way too low. This is because in reality their offer would have been more like 40% below market value, and the repossession company would have probably continued to keep marketing it to get more. I knew that had I not offered what I did then the property would have been marketed further, and more than likely achieved a lot more than what was paid and I would have lost out. The fact I knew my market and could complete quickly meant that I was able to offer what is close to asking price, but still well below market value.

2. Priced to sell

The other way this happens is when a property comes to the market that is priced to sell by the agent. Now let me ask you a question here. Let's say an agent goes to view a property so they can list it and start marketing it for the vendor. Now if they go round and value it at 100k and then let the vendor know that they will list it at this, do you think they are likely to take an offer straight away of £80-85k?

The answer I'm sure you will agree is probably no, especially in a stronger market. However as mentioned earlier properties can be over-valued by agents to get a listing, and similarly they can be under-valued if the vendor has told the agent they want a quick sale and are motivated to move. Remember that a vendor's motivation is not always the price, and an agent would rather show someone round they know is serious about buying, than have to do lots of viewings instead. This means that sometimes an agent can do some of the work for you as they may speak to the vendor and tell them that although their property make be worth £100k they do not know how long it would take to sell at this, and so to gain interest they should market it around £90k. If you then view the property and offer £80-85k then this has a far better chance of being accepted, and although it seems like it is only a bit off the asking price, it is actually more of a discount off the actual value.

Timing

Now this is very important and is a key factor to making money when you buy. It can actually be the most important factor in a lot of cases.

> Important note: It has been said if you 'do the right thing at the wrong time you get pain' which can be the case.

Timing also covers a lot, from being in the right place at the right time through to being quick to make an offer on a property before anyone else gets there.

There are many examples of when timing has been very important to me but one particular example springs to mind from a while ago. A property came to market and I was trying to get access with a particular agent. There were no details on the property but the agent had given me an idea of what it would be coming on the market for, and when the first viewings would be done. They told me that there was a group viewing that was being done on Tuesday at 11am and that was the first chance that it could be done. Because I never like to assume things, I asked the agent if they could get me in earlier. They were initially hesitant but again as I do not like to give up, I asked again, and they eventually said that they would see if the vendor was available to show me round before. I actually managed to get in the evening before to view the property and then was able to make an offer of near what the agent said was acceptable and the offer was accepted and the sale was agreed. Now had I gone round only the following morning for the group viewing I may have been outbid, and there would have been a lot more competition. I agreed this property partly due to the relationship I had with the agent, but mainly because I pressed the agent for further information, and most importantly because I dropped everything else I was doing to get round there, as I knew that timing was everything. It can also be the case that a vendor may have had a sale fall through a number of times, and so sometimes outside influences can help and luck can be on your side.

This just proves how important timing is. I often have seen investors chase properties when the timing is not right and this can lead to a lot of time being burnt with no result.

Similarly, I have also had many other times when I have met important clients or business partners and it has often been about timing.

There is a saying 'Luck is when opportunity meets preparedness'. There are some people who will say you were lucky to get these opportunities. I don't agree with this as whilst you may have been fortunate to get the break, there is no luck in the fact you are putting yourself in the right places and are prepared to take your opportunities when they arise. This is all about timing and building your knowledge.

Summary: Making money from day one when you buy the property is key. This will set you up from the outset and give you a buffer as well. It is not always straightforward to get the exact market value as you may get differing views from different parties. You can however do as much research as possible as mentioned above to get the actual facts which is what we are looking for. It is also important to realise that asking price is not always value and so you need to know your market well to distinguish the two, as there are often different valuations of the same asset from different people.

6. PROPERTY IS A BUSINESS AND NEEDS TO BE TREATED LIKE ONE FROM DAY ONE

Property should always be treated as a business from day one, so you can achieve optimum results and income, whether part time or full time. If you treat property investing as a pastime or hobby then it will likely repay you in this way. If you treat it a business from day one then the possibilities of what you can achieve are endless.

You will have already heard the saying "you make your money when you buy", which is true. Buying property at a discount is vitally important, but so is buying property for cash flow. Cash flow makes you financially free and is what will pay you monthly in your property business. Especially in a time when capital growth is slow, buying for cash flow gives you security and minimises your risk. When the income from your property business flows well, it will allow you to free up your time and have a healthy income to live. You may also wish to re-invest some of this positive cash flow which will add another string to your bow.

As mentioned earlier, the cash flow from a property is measured by taking the rent and then subtracting all the expenses, including the mortgage payment, insurance, management fees (if applicable), and maintenance costs. The excess money is positive cash flow that you can deposit in the bank after your tax is paid. I personally always look for at least £200 per month cash flow on all my property purchases. This I feel is the absolute least an investor should be looking for in the current climate. Before the property crash in 2008 a lot of investors were happy with a property to 'wash its face', and as long as it did not cost them monthly they were happy. This was down to the fact they were anticipating capital growth and so rental income and yield were not so important to them.

Things have certainly changed in recent years and cash flow is vitally important in the current climate, and is now what savvy investors are focusing on. Property is essentially a long term game, and it is a medium to long term investment. If you are planning on keeping your buy-to-let properties for at least five to ten years, which I believe you should, then it is likely you will see capital growth in this time. Buying properties that cash flow well means that you can make a solid income monthly from your portfolio and not have to just wait and rely on this capital increase.

Case study one: One of the first buy to lets that I bought

One of the first buy to let properties I bought was in 2008 and I feel it is a good example of buying a property and treating it as a business from day one, and the value of this. Now this property was purchased just as the recession started and so I wasn't expecting capital growth anytime soon. I was investing however for cash flow and for income purposes. My aim was to stress test the investment so that it not only worked at the time I bought it, but as the years went on as well therefore minimising my risk and giving my investment longevity. This was treating the property as a business from day one.

I purchased the property for £67000 and it was rented out for £525 per month. After the Mortgage payment and all other costs, the Cash flow per month was £273.

Now for a single let property in my area that gave me a healthy cash flow per month which I was happy with, and it gave me a good addition to my portfolio. But I wanted to stress test the investment as someone would in another business to protect themselves from a change of circumstances in the future and so I asked myself many questions to protect myself such as:

1. What happens when interest rates rise?
2. What happens if I want to re-mortgage the property?
3. Is there an opportunity for rents to rise In the future?

Now I knew that it was likely interest rates would rise in the future and so my aim was to be proactive and not get any nasty surprises. After assessing these questions and scenarios I came to the conclusion that even when rates rise, and I re-mortgaged the property, it would be still be cash flow positive and so I realised that it was a good solid investment. It was also in an area that had strong rental potential and so there would likely be opportunity to increase the rents on a yearly or bi-yearly basis as well. All in all it ticked many boxes, and it is how I like to treat all potential purchases so that I cover as many bases as possible.

> Important tip: Every property should be treated as a business. It should have its own separate file and spreadsheet and the profitability should be reviewed regularly over time.

Summary: It is so important that you give property investing respect and treat it as a business from day 1. Failure to do so will likely result in you not getting the results you require. Each property you buy should be treated as a mini business in its own right, and that way you will be able to see the true profitability of each investment and therefore reach your goals quicker.

7. DON'T LET LOW SOLD PRICES PUT YOU OFF INVESTING

One of the biggest mistakes I feel I have seen new investors make when new to property is that they solely rely on sold prices when making a decision on the value of a property. This can be a financially fatal mistake, and mean that you potentially could leave thousands of pounds on the table.

Now I am certainly not saying that sold prices should not be looked at, however it should only be one thing in a list of other things that you do when researching whether a property is a good buy.

A really good example of this is a property that I purchased back in 2009. It was a 2-bed flat about ten minutes from town and I still remember getting the call to this day. It was from somebody looking to sell their property within 14 days and so the essence of speed and timing was very apparent here. I got the call one afternoon and as always made an appointment to go out and view the property. The property, if I am honest, was not in the best area of town but I still wanted to go out and have a look to make my own conclusion. After viewing the property I was pleasantly surprised and it did not seem as bad as I had been told. (That is another lesson I learned, to always make your own mind up and not listen to the stereotypes as they are not always true). I made my way home and began to go through the rigorous due diligence that I go through with every property I look at. I told the vendor that I would call back within the next 24 hours with an offer for the property which I subsequently did. After doing my due diligence I realised that I could only pay a maximum of £25,500k for the property if it was to be a cash sale. This was based on this fact, and also the level of refurbishment that was needed to get the property to the required rental standard. The vendor informed me that he would accept this offer if I could do it within the 14 days, preferably before. This was because he had some debts he wished to pay off and wanted a lump sum to contribute to another property he was buying with his partner. I also agreed to pay his legal fees for the purchase so he would walk away with the agreed amount and not have other costs involved.

This worked out as a win/win situation for both, which I mentioned earlier was such an important thing to remember. There was actually another sale on the property next to mine in the block and this property actually went for £38,000, rather than the £25,500 I had paid for mine. The benefit of knowing your area well and others around is that you can get information from other sources and I was told on the grapevine that this was actually another investor buying this property. This made me realise once again that sold prices were not the only thing to rely on as they do not always show the full story or the full value of the property. Because the investor was experienced, he knew he was still buying a discounted asset at 38k with a high yield as the property was worth £50-55k in good condition. He was still going to make a very good return. Had he relied on just the sold prices then he may have walked away as mine was lower, not really knowing the true circumstances behind the sale. Had he done this he would have lost out on a very good investment himself. Sometimes there are anomalies and sold prices are lower, especially in areas where it has mainly been investors buying.

Summary: The sold price is just one aspect when trying to work out the value of a property. When there is a downturn in the market, it is likely that sold prices at the lower end of the market will be low due to the fact that it is investors who are mainly buying. Use this as a guide and not an absolute view of value as these properties are often bought at a discount already, and the property may still be a good investment even if there are sold prices lower than yours.

8. YOU WILL NEED TO LEARN HOW TO SUCCESSFULLY MANAGE YOUR CASH FLOW

Property is like any other business, and to be successful you will need to learn how to manage your cash flow. The key is to take into consideration all costs at the start to make sure there are no hidden surprises along the way. This will help you predict and manage cash flow more successfully.

On a rental property you will need to think about many things such as mortgage payments, insurances, and any service or management charges that apply. I also personally factor in 10% of the rent as an incidental fund on all properties. Over my years in property taking this extra 10% has typically been enough to cover any maintenance and repairs on my properties. For example on a property where the rent is £500 per month, I allocate £50 per month which would give £600 per year for the property. Barring a major problem such as a boiler replacement, I have found this to be enough as an average to cover other repairs and safety checks that are legally required.

With regards to the bigger jobs such as boilers, I have always looked at the condition of these when factoring in how much the refurbishment will be on the property. If the boiler looks old, then this is a good bargaining tool and you should be looking to factor this in when you make an offer on how much you are willing to pay. By factoring in this incidental fund you can manage cash flow well, but also build and keep a pot for when things need doing, so you will not get caught short.

This is key as, to be successful in property, we need to make sure we service our debt, and if we do this then over time our assets grow and build.

The concept of good and bad debt, was something that I didn't understand before I got into property. It is something that is talked about a lot in the property investment and the business world, and for very good reason as the richest and most successful people out there understand this and use the concept very well.

So what is the difference between the two?

Bad debts are those that drain your wealth, are not affordable and offer no real prospect of 'paying for themselves' in the future.

Bad debts are also likely to have no realistic repayment plans, and are often run up when people make impulse purchases of items they don't really need, or borrow money to pay everyday bills.

If you can't afford to borrow the money (for example, you aren't sure you'll be able to make the monthly repayments) it is definitely a bad debt.

In simple terms, a good debt is one that is a sensible investment in your financial future, should leave you better off in the long-term and should not have a negative impact on your overall financial position.

You will have a clear and specific reason for taking it out, and a realistic plan for paying it back that allows you to clear the debt as quickly as possible, or in a series of regular and affordable payments (for example a mortgage).

Someone with a good debt will also have identified the cheapest possible way of borrowing that money. They will have done this by finding the borrowing method, an interest rate, loan or credit amount term and charges that are the most appropriate for them. In some cases it will mean a deal with the lowest possible interest rate, but for others it may not, for example if the lowest rate comes with the price of high charges or penalties which some may not want.

So managing your debt accordingly and making sure you have control of this has fantastic benefits over time. This is especially so with mortgage interest because inflation erodes this over time, meaning your debt decreases as values rise.

Learning this concept and theory not only changed my view but also my financial life accordingly. It is something that I stress to people nowadays as it is vital to your success.

So how much cash flow can I expect from each property?

This does really depend on the purchase price of the property and the rent that can be achieved. The rent that can be achieved varies dramatically around the country, and I often hear potential investors complain that investments just don't stack up where they live.

Whilst I would agree that it is possible that investments may not stack up exactly where you live, I would suggest that there is almost certainly somewhere within an hour of where you live where the rents will stack up. This will then become your goldmine area as discussed earlier.

What if investments do not stack up?

If investments do not stack up in your area, then this is the point when you will want to look for another area to invest for the purposes of buy to let. Again this is an important point about area in that the area you live in may not work for a buy-to-let strategy. It may however be a hotspot where people like to live and therefore there could be opportunities to buy properties, add value and then sell for a profit. Whilst I am not an advocate of too many different areas, often investors may have a couple of areas which work for different strategies. It is important to test the area first, and then if you do have to go further afield (within 45 minutes preferably) then at least you will know, and will have made an informed decision based on the evidence you have gathered.

Personally where I live in the West Midlands, a mid-terrace property with three bedrooms would cost anywhere between £85,000 and £120,000 depending on the area. Now obviously there are three bedroom properties that are worth a lot more that, but I am just focusing on the specific area that I have highlighted for investment.

Now let's look at these purely as investment vehicles:

The 3-bedroom property at £120,000 would likely rent at £625 as a single-let property. If you were to take a 75% mortgage on the property then the mortgage advance would be £90,000. If you were to have a mortgage with an interest rate of 5% my calculations would suggest that you have interest payments of approximately £400 per month once other mortgage fees had been added on. If you then add on insurances, potential management charges, and a maintenance contingency you would be doing well to come out with a monthly cash flow of around £100 per month. Now this is not really a lot to get excited about in the scheme of things.

At this monthly profit, how many of these properties would you need to replace your monthly income? You may find that it is a lot more than you would wish to own.

So that is why I would focus on the property at £90,000 (even if it is not as pretty to look at) and let's see why.

The property at £90,000 in my area, would rent for £575 per month, so less than the property at £120,000. With that being said, the returns are still higher and let's see how.

At £90,000 again assuming a loan to value of 75% you would require a mortgage advance of £67,500. Again if you had an interest rate of 5% you would have interest payments of approximately £290 per month. If you then add on insurances, potential management charges, and a maintenance contingency you would be looking to come out with a monthly cash flow of around £200 per month, which is more the level I am looking for with my single-let investments. I am always looking for cash flow that is at least this amount, as it gives a healthy amount each property.

Should I have an incidental fund or re-invest all the cash flow?

This is a question I am asked regularly by people that are starting out in property and are beginning to buy their first assets. Now I would certainly not tell anyone how to spend the cash flow they are making, but I find that I always like an incidental fund available, and it helps keep the business in a healthy cash flow position. You may decide to re-invest profits in the future once there is a healthy amount in the pot. This is what I have done in the past, but I always like to keep some money aside in case maintenance is needed on a property.

Keeping void periods down to a minimum so they don't affect cash flow

Voids periods are unfortunately something that we all need to accept when we get into property. Many people are in denial about voids though. This can happen a lot when certain individuals or companies try to source properties on to others, giving all their figures based on there being no void periods throughout the year at all.

The reality is that all voids will eat into your profit. You need to know the number of days, as an average, that your properties are vacant every single month and every single year.

Managing your cash flow is so important because, although we all know that we will get capital growth over time which we want, if you can't manage and get the cash flow right from day one, then there's a very good chance that the negative cash flow could finish you, especially if you decide to increase the size of your portfolio to 20, 50, or even 100 plus properties. As a general rule, many professional investors do their figures based on two months void a year. Based on this, if the property still gives you a good return, then this should be a sufficient buffer.

You can however multiply your cash flow using a multi-let strategy and this is explained in further detail later in the book. Again you still need to be aware of your cash flow figures as there are extra costs associated with this as compared to a single let, but we will be covering this further in another chapter.

Summary: Successfully managing your cash flow is vital to your success. To be successful in property investment you will need to service your debt, and for that you need cash flow coming into your business. Keep an eye on your cash flow regularly to make sure that it is in order, and always keep an incidental fund available for a rainy day.

9. THE IMPORTANCE OF NOT RELYING ON ONE INCOME STREAM

This is a key lesson I have learned along my journey from some very rich and successful people, and I feel that it is a very important aspect for somebody to achieve their true potential and minimise their risk. When new to property or looking to invest initially you may feel that you just want to buy a few properties to begin to make a passive income. You may not understand the fact that there are many strategies available out there in property for you to discover, I certainly didn't when I started out. As you begin to invest and learn more about successful investors and business entrepreneurs, you will soon realise that they do not rely on one income stream entirely and have multiple ways of generating income. This can be in a variety of ways such as different property strategies that generate income, or through separate businesses that they control.

Now it is important to remember here that there are many property strategies available to use, and below is an example of some of these strategies, with some being more advanced than others.

Buying property yourself

This is the most obvious place to start and for the novice investor they believe that property investment ends there: 'If I don't have the money sitting in my bank account then it ends there doesn't it?' 'I can't make money from property surely?'

Well the reality is that there are many other strategies to make income from property even if you do not buy them yourself, or currently do not have the money yourself to buy. They will be explained further in this chapter but for now let's look at the first most obvious way of generating income from property investment which is buying property yourself.

When I started to invest in property I wanted to own property myself and build a large portfolio. Now whilst this is not a bad thing to want to do, I quickly realised that unless I had an extremely rich friend or family member who was willing to back me (which unfortunately was not the case) there would only be a certain amount of properties that I could buy myself before all my own funds had been invested. With that being said, I thought that I would start buying property myself and then look at other strategies alongside this as well. Therefore if you are in a position to buy you can start to invest in buy to let investments, or look at buying and selling property as your main strategy.

Different ways to get deposit finance

There are many different ways to attract finance if you are starting out in property. During this section you will find out many different ways to buy property using other people's money and also other cash flow strategies that do not require much start-up capital. This means you can still profit and make money through property. However it is always worth looking to see if you have any resources available, as you then have the option to buy with your own funds as well, thereby retaining more of the profits.

You can initially look at whether you have any savings in the bank or equity in any property that you could release to be used for deposits. Many people don't like the idea of using equity in their own home to invest as they see this as very risky. If this is how you feel, I would like you to think again as the equity in your home could allow you to pay off your home mortgage a lot sooner and become financially free.

As an example let's assume you've got some equity in your home. For many years you have been working hard to pay off your home mortgage, and you are happy that the amount you owe is decreasing. If you are only ever going to have one property (the home you live in) then it is a very good idea to pay off your home mortgage as quickly as you possibly can. By paying off your home mortgage you will be reducing one of your biggest outgoing expenses and you will reach financial independence far more quickly. However, investors think differently about this.

Many people are content to pay off the mortgage because they believe that over time, the value of their asset will increase. If your home is worth £100,000 now then you could just sit back and relax and in 10 years' time your property will probably double in value to £200,000, based on historical data. This would make you feel good as you may well feel that you are financially better off because your house has increased in value, but really in reality you are no better off. You see, all the other properties will also have gone up in value as well.

If you wanted to move from your existing house to a similar sized house that would also cost you £200,000. In real terms you've had no net gain. And for you to benefit from that increase in value you would have to sell the house and downsize to a smaller, cheaper property or move to a cheaper area which is what many people do when they retire in order to release some cash.

Investors recognise that it's beneficial to have more than one property because they can profit from the increased capital value of multiple properties.

Therefore instead of trying to pay off their own home as quickly as possible, investors have a different mind-set and think in a different way. Where they can they will use equity from their existing property or properties to buy more to expand their portfolio.

Therefore someone with an investor's mind set would look to take the other route. Let's say for the purposes of this example that someone has a property worth £100,000 and they want to invest in other properties. They could potentially release up to 80% of the value and therefore if they wanted to they could release £80,000. The amount someone wants to release would be down to them and their risk profile, but for this example we will assume that they release £80,000.

I will base the example on properties in my area, and with this £80000 you could likely purchase an extra three properties, and comfortably have money for any refurbishment, legal fees and other costs.

To keep the example simple we will also assume the BTL (Buy to let) properties you would purchase are worth about £100,000 in today's market.

Therefore if you bought 3 extra properties you would then have four properties that potentially would double in value over time. If you purchased the other three properties using a 20% deposit then you would have three properties that have an £80,000 mortgage on each. You would therefore owe £240,000 to the bank but have three assets that are worth £300,000 in total. Assuming those properties double in value over a period of time based on historical data, then the value of each property would be £200,000. You would then have three properties worth £600,000 and still have the £240,000 debt, meaning you have £360,000 worth of equity in those three properties. The original property you borrowed against has doubled as well to £200,000 and you have a loan of £80,000 against this. Therefore you have £120,000 worth of equity in this property, and so the four together are worth £800,000 and have £480,000 equity in total. You can either stop there or repeat the process again building even further.

If you had only had one property that was paid off completely then you would have a portfolio worth £200,000 with no debt and so have £200,000 worth of equity. Now as stated earlier, if you do not like the idea of this then you should aim to pay off your home mortgage as quickly as possible, but this is just an example to show how investing can increase your wealth significantly. If you are using other people's money to do this as well, then you are getting an infinite return.

That is also not taking into consideration the cash flow from the properties you will get as you go along, which is vitally important because 'cash flow is king'. You would need to understand that you will have a debt to service from the original property you have refinanced. Therefore as an example if by releasing the original £80,000 it costs you £300 per month you will want to make sure that the three properties you buy cash flow well in excess of this, which is all down to your upfront due diligence, which as highlighted in the book is extremely important.

Alternative sources of deposit finance

If you do not have any equity available or do not want to use this then you could think about people you know who may have some equity. You may have family and friends who have plenty of equity and would like to invest in property but have no idea how to do it. You could joint venture with them whereby you put in the time and effort and they provide the seed capital for deposits (we will be covering Joint venture and other cash flow strategies further in this chapter)

There is also Inheritance which is another option. Do you have any inheritance that you have been left, or have your parents got equity in their own home that will one day come your way?

Would it be possible to get some of that money in advance? If they give you some money and then live for at least another seven years, the gift would be considered to be outside of their estate and so would avoid any inheritance tax liability.

Alternatively, where else could you borrow money from? Could you take out a private loan? This was something I did in the past. I was able to borrow money at 6% and make a better return than 6% from the investment property I bought with that loan money. This may not be for everyone but it is another way. It is about thinking outside the box, and looking at all of your options.

There are many different ways to find the deposits. The key here is to remember you want to use as little of your own money as possible if you can.

You can also buy multiple properties using one deposit. This occurs when you add value to a property and have it re-valued, or when the market increases and you have it re-valued. You can then take the equity out to buy more property. (This is covered more in the leverage section)

I began to use the other strategies explained in this chapter as well, which you can use currently if you are not in a position to buy yourself.

The key point here is that whilst there are many strategies available it is important to master one before moving on. There are however huge possibilities out there for you when you have systemised one strategy and want to move on to the next. So what are these different strategies?

Sourcing properties for others

This proved to be a very beneficial strategy for me over the years and has allowed me to help many other investors become financially free as well as myself, which has proved very rewarding. As I began my journey in property and began to buy properties for myself I quickly realised that I would run out of funds at some point. This is a very important point to remember in the fact that no matter how much money you have in property, you always run out. Even for investors that have millions of pounds they may be looking for extra investment to do even bigger deals, and so using different cash flow strategies is key.

I actually fell into property sourcing and deal packaging by accident in some respects. It was 2009 and I had bought a handful of properties myself, and because of the tough economic times I was finding bank finance tougher and tougher to get as things had tightened up due to the recession we were in. This brought frustration in itself, as because of the relationships I had built with agents I was beginning to get more property leads through than I could personally buy myself. After surrounding myself with other people in the property industry I found out about property sourcing for others which allowed me to build another cash flowing strategy into my business which was fantastic. I was able to keep my relationships with agents as I was still able to buy properties through introducing other people so they were happy, and I then had another income stream so it was win/win for everybody. I then continued to build my portfolio alongside deal packaging, which gave me a business for cash flow, and the property purchases for asset building.

So what is property sourcing and deal packaging and how does it work?

It is where you, as the property investor, source suitable investment properties for clients who are cash rich but time poor. You will then be able to charge a fee for this and also provide add-on services should the client want these. This in a nutshell, is what 'Deal Packaging' is, however there are many component parts which is what we will highlight here.

Why is deal packaging such a good strategy?

Deal Packaging is a fantastic strategy to use, both when starting out in property and also as you become more experienced. This is for a variety of reasons, one of the main ones being that you do not need large amounts of start-up capital yourself. This can be very appealing for somebody new who is looking to get into property, either alongside building their own portfolio or simply by using this strategy as a way to set up their own property business. When systemized and done correctly this is a great strategy to either generate a part-time or even full-time income. Now this might not be something you wish to do now, but it is something that you can do if you are in a position where you cannot currently buy. I often hear investors or people looking to get into property say, "There is no point researching or viewing property as I cannot buy it myself!" Well this strategy dispels that myth because you can still research your area, and find profitable properties for others. By doing this you can start your journey in property and also become a very 'investable concept' which will be very attractive to potential joint venture and other business partners.

Single lets vs multi-lets

When I first started out in property I had only planned on buying rental property to let out to families on a single let tenancy. This was the strategy I initially used and I am certainly a fan of single let properties and these are a big part of my business. As I started out buying these properties however, and after meeting other property investors, I realised that there was also the multi-let (HMO) strategy.

What is a multi-let or HMO?

A multi-let property is where a property is rented out

individually by the room. The actual definition is a property let to 3 or more 'unrelated' people, who all share kitchen and bathroom facilities.

Multi-letting a property is a fantastic way to boost cash flow in your business and is certainly a popular strategy with property investors today. Rental demand is high in many areas as many people save to get on the housing ladder when they get the chance to do so. However, they still need somewhere to live in the meantime and this is why multi-lets are a popular strategy to use.

This is because financially you can certainly achieve a lot more rent than with a standard single let property. For example let's take a standard 3 bedroom house in my goldmine area. Renting this out in a standard way as a single let you would likely achieve anywhere from £550-£600 per month. Instead of renting this property to a family, you could rent the property out to four different people paying in the region of £350 per month per room. This is provided it is the right kind of property with three bedrooms and two reception rooms. This is important as one of the reception rooms could potentially be used as a bedroom, giving you four renting units. This would give a total monthly rent of £1400 per month on this basis, and so you can see why it is an attractive proposition.

If you like the idea of renting out your properties on a multi-let basis to maximise your cash flow, there are a number of things you will need to consider first.

The property location

Location is always important when you buy a property, but particularly with a multi-let property. You will need to make sure that the property is in an area where your target tenants would like to live. In my area there are particular hot spots where students or young professionals would like to live. The things to often consider will be things such as public transport links, local facilities and amenities, and the location to places of work or universities, depending on whether it is students or young professionals you are aiming at.

The size of the rooms

In all of my multi-let properties I want to make sure that the majority of the rooms are double rooms with good space for a double bed and all the other things needed such as wardrobes and chest of drawers. That is not to say that single rooms will not work, I have just found personally that double rooms rent quicker and young professionals and students prefer to be in double beds. To make sure your rooms fit the required size, I would always recommend speaking to your local council to get the minimum room sizes required. Dependant on the amount of rooms and people in the house, you may also be able to put couples in some of the bigger rooms, potentially getting more cash flow this way as well. You will need to make sure you do not exceed the amount of people allowed before needing a licence or planning permission.

The number of rooms

As all of the utility bills are often included in the rent, it is important to make sure you have at least four rentable rooms per property to spread the cost of the monthly bills. These bills include things such as the council tax, water rates, and gas and electric amongst others. In my area, I have found that I need at least four rooms to make multi-lets a viable proposition, and then if I have five rooms it starts to become even more profitable.

HMO licensing

Multi-letting a property can require a licence in some cases. This is when a property has five or more tenants on three or more floors. If you are operating a HMO property which requires mandatory licencing then you will need to apply to your local council for a HMO licence. The process is fairly straight forward, but can be time consuming. You complete the forms and submit them with your application fee, which currently in my council is £776.25 for seven units/lets. There is an additional fee of £10.50 per unit/person over seven units/lets, however you will need to check these prices in your chosen area. Your property will then be inspected at some point to make sure it meets all the relevant standards. It is important to remember that whether your multi-let property needs to be licenced or not, it still needs to adhere to the current safety standards required regarding things such as fire doors, emergency exits, emergency lighting etc. I always recommend that you contact your local council to seek guidance to ensure that you are providing suitable safe accommodation for your tenants. You can also contact a local fire officer who should be able to come out and give you a report on fire safety, and advice on what needs to be done to comply.

Article 4

Article 4 is also something you need to consider if you are going to pursue a multi-let strategy. This means that planning permission is required before a dwelling or house is altered to a House in Multiple Occupation (HMO). If you are looking at the multi-let strategy then I would certainly find out first if the area you are looking at has Article 4, as you will want to find this out in advance.

Single lets and multi-lets are two fantastic strategies which both have merits and certain drawbacks. As long as you are aware of these you will be able to decide which strategy suits you better at any given time.

What are the differences between the two?

In my opinion the main differences between the two are:

Single let:

1. They are potentially longer tenancies
2. Lower cash flow and rents
3. Less upfront cost- Lower purchase price
4. Less Maintenance/management
5. Potentially an easier sale as the property is not converted
6. There are often more mortgage options
7. You can often recycle your deposit easier if you wish

Multi-let:

1. Higher tenant turnover
2. Higher cash flow
3. Higher purchase price
4. More maintenance/management
5. Potentially harder sale
6. Attractive sale to investors
7. Usually less mortgage options – potentially using commercial finance

Now this is not to say that this will always be the case, but in my experience I have found this to be the main differences the majority of the time. In addition to this there are also often other costs required with a multi-let and therefore you need to be aware of these to stay compliant. These can be things such as Furniture, Fire Doors, Extra Smoke Alarms, Fire Officer/Council officer inspection, and Stud/Partition Walls.

The two strategies certainly both work and it is personal preference on which one investors will use. I always think a mixture of the two works well, with many people new to property starting out with single let properties. From here they can then move onto multi-lets as they get more experienced. If you are looking to start with a multi-let strategy then adhering to the above will stand you in good stead, and it is important to understand all the costs so that you are not caught short.

The buy to sell strategy

I personally like to hold property for the long term as a general rule, although I have bought and sold property in the past. Buying and selling property is often a very popular strategy with current investors, or new people coming to the market, as you can potentially make good profits in a relatively short space of time. You may have seen the various television programmes which bring this strategy to light, showing the people who renovate property and then sell on for a profit, known as 'flipping' property. It tends to be a buzz word and I have heard many people say that they would like to buy a property, do it up, and sell it on for a £15-20k profit. Now I can certainly see why as that is a very appealing proposition, as you may agree, especially when it may only take a few months!

Now like I said as a general rule when I buy property I like to hold onto it for the long term. I don't really like to sell just to make short term cash although I have done in the past. The tax implications can also sometimes be greater with a flip depending on your situation as it is classed as trading, but it is important as mentioned to consult a qualified tax specialist if this is your chosen strategy.

There are however, as with every other strategy, things you need to do to ensure that you are minimising your risk, and giving yourself the best chance of making a good profit. What you often may not hear about are the horror stories where people have tried this and unfortunately been stung and not made any profit, or in worst cases it has actually cost them money. This would likely have been because they have not followed some core fundamentals when flipping property. Buying and selling property can be a fantastic strategy, and one I have used myself successfully, but it is important to remember the following points:

1. Make sure you get enough of a discount or considerable value can be added

To buy and flip a property you need to be purchasing it at a big enough discount. This is because to make any money you need to get a big enough discount to cover the purchase costs, sale costs, holding costs, and allow for the property to be sold on to the end-consumer at a small discount. I would suggest that you are looking to buy a property at least 25% below the true market value, but preferably 30% to add a contingency. Interestingly enough though there are other ways to get this discount other than from just the initial sale price. As mentioned earlier, when buying and selling property, you can often make money through doing refurbishment work. Now whilst I would not recommend big structural projects if you are new (unless you are a builder or know a good one you can trust), you can be looking to buy run-down properties which need refurbishment work such as new kitchen, bathroom, double glazing, and carpeting and decoration throughout. By doing this you can create and add the value. A mistake new investors sometimes make is looking for properties that look nice and everything is done. I always like to add value even with buy to let purchases, as it is a good negotiating tool, but with buying and selling it is key. For example I purchased a property recently for £70,000 that was worth £80,000-£85,000 in its current condition but was in a bad state of repair. I knew that by spending seven to ten thousand pounds, the property would then be worth in the region of £105,000 and so it would work for me, and make a good profit on the back end. Looking at properties that are run down and tired is key with this strategy, as often properties that are already new and modern will be marketed for maximum price and get more attention from first time buyers. The run down properties will often not be as popular and competition is less. By understanding your market and knowing what you know now, you can then be the one to cash in on these that others may not want, or not know what to do with.

2. Make sure you can cover the holding costs

When buying and selling, the property may take a while to sell on the open market. You can look to minimise this time by informing the agent early on, possibly while the property is being refurbished if it needs this. Until the property is sold, you will have to cover all of the holding costs such as interest payments on a mortgage, insurances, and maybe council tax or other bills. The longer it takes to sell the property, the higher your holding costs will be so you need to make sure you have enough cash flow to cover these costs.

3. Use a great proactive estate agent

The time it takes to sell your property can depend on the quality of the estate agent you use. Selecting the right estate agent is vital. You want to look for an agent who is proactive not reactive, and has a list of buyers looking for the type of property that you have to sell. A good agent should be able to advise you on the price at which you need to put the property on the market to achieve a quick sale. If you are looking to find an agent to sell a property for you then there are many questions I would be asking them such as:

- How many properties have you sold in the area recently?
- Do you have people who are currently looking in the area?

- What is your average time taken to sell a property currently?
- What is the length of your estate agency agreement that I am contracted to?

I would also not sign a contract that is either too long or sign exclusively with one agent. You want to give yourself the best chance of selling quickly and so to have multiple agents is a good idea, and should then avoid complacency as well, which could happen if there is only one agent.

4. Make sure your property has the 'kerb appeal'

When selling a property it is vitally important to give the property the 'wow factor.' You will be looking to sell on to a homeowner or a first time buyer, and therefore you will want to make sure the property appeals the minute they walk through the door. This will often mean going that step further than if you were going to rent the property out. For example when we rent properties out, whilst they are all done to the required standard and are in good condition, it can differ from when we sell a property. To give your property the wow factor you may decide to go further with your refurbishment works. Therefore as an example instead of putting in a trade kitchen, you may decide to put a better quality kitchen and bathroom in to get interest. You may decide to make an open plan kitchen diner style, which is very popular currently in certain areas. You may also want to dress the property for viewings and make sure the décor and carpets are all new, amongst other things. You will need to check with your local agent to make sure this will give you the return you require, but often going that step further when selling a property is key. Putting yourself in the shoes of the buyer is essential. Often people buying property to live in do not want big refurbishment projects. Therefore by making it appealing and homely, it will likely sell quicker on the open market.

Joint ventures

It was back in 2010 when I was first introduced to a joint venture and quickly realised the power of these. I had been investing for about two years and had come to the point where I had invested all of my own deposit funds. Now as stated earlier this happens to many investors no matter how much money you happen to start out with. It is also important to learn that this is not the end of the road and from attending property networking events, researching and meeting with other successful investors I found out about Joint venture partnerships.

So what is a Joint venture?

A Joint venture (JV) is a business agreement in which parties agree to develop a new entity, by each party contributing assets, equity, skills, experience, and power team.

It is not always about doing property Joint ventures together, Joint ventures can take many different forms which

I will explain more about in this chapter.

To become a really successful investor you will need to think bigger than just what you can do on your own. Working with other investors in joint ventures can give you access to more investment opportunities, and a greater variety as well. I have found that Joint ventures can give you:

- Access to knowledge and experience
- Money to fund projects
- Time to find great deals
- A better network of suppliers and contacts.

A JV partner is also not necessarily someone who just has money, but a mixture of the following traits:

- Complementary skill sets: for example one partner is an expert marketer in exchange for the other partner's mortgageability and/or management skills.
- Cash & Time: One partner is cash-rich, but time-poor; the other partner is time-rich, but cash-poor.
- Time & Experience. One partner has lots of experience, but little time; the other partner has lots of time, but little experience.
- Experience & Cash: one partner has lots of experience but no cash; the other has lots of cash but no experience.
- Contacts: It is important to remember that your 'network' is your 'net-worth' and so you may want to

bring in a JV partner for their contacts and the people they can put you in touch with.

This can be very beneficial over time as this makes the most of leverage so that there is no limit to what you can achieve with the right partners. (This is also explained in the Leverage section of the book).

What are some of the ways you can invest with other people?

There are many different ways to invest with people. Some of the main ways people invest together are:

- Buying property together where you are both on the mortgage
- Buying property cash where one or both parties put the money up.
- Buying property through a company with multiple directors

These are just some of the ways and I would always advise to get the relevant legal, financial and tax advice on what is right for you if you decide to pursue this route.

As mentioned Joint ventures can also happen in different ways. People often ask about Joint ventures and think it is just about doing property deals or projects together. Whilst this is a fantastic way to move forward with your property business, there are other ways to use joint venture relationships. I remember speaking to someone and we were discussing Joint ventures and working with other people. He mentioned that he was currently working with someone to generate property leads online. He mentioned that he had met someone who said that they knew how to market for property online but had limited funds. Therefore they agreed that one would pay for the advertising and the other would market for the leads, and that they would split what came in accordingly to pass onto their investors. This is just one example of how it can be a different type of Joint venture. Many people set up networking events together, or do email list swaps together, to help market each other's business. This is not necessarily a property purchasing Joint venture, but is a business joint venture which could be focused on marketing, training or mentoring, or their management and letting businesses. It is an important point to remember that making good solid contacts can help in many ways, and the key is to look at your strengths and find opposing skillsets to complement each other.

What are Joint venture partners looking for from you?

Obviously you be will rejected by a few investors which is normal and you will want to make sure you are rejection proof, but if you keep repeating the process you will manage to find a lot of qualified JV partners and a big database full of cash rich investors whom you can email or ring for finance as soon as you find a good Below Market Value [BMV] property that needs their cash injection.

Some of the main things investors will be looking for in you will be:

Credibility

A potential Joint Venture partner will almost certainly be looking for credibility from you. Interestingly enough, credibility may not always mean the amount of properties you have in your portfolio. A common thought is that this may be the case, however one of my first Joint Venture partners said to me that they found me to have credibility because of my knowledge of my investment area. Finding and researching your own investment area is key when looking to become credible and investable.

To not be pushy

A potential partner will definitely not want you to be pushy about your idea or offer. This is almost certainly going to be a complete turn off for a potential investor. You will want to build rapport and build a personal relationship with that person first. People work with people they know, like and trust and this should be your goal from the outset. For example, you should not be pushing a property deal under someone's nose straight away at a property meet. You should be talking to that person on a general level first, and then aim to have a one to one meeting with them to understand their long-term goals.

Regular inclusion and updates – should they want this

Including your investment partner in the property deal and

liaising with them regularly will be of great value to them. Agreeing from day one that the other person will also be able to play a part in the decisions that are made allows them to feel secure and trust you with their money. This of course is as long as being included in the property side of the investment is something they want, as not all partners have the time, or will want to do so. The key is to find out how included they wish to be.

An exit strategy

A Joint Venture partner will want to know what their exit strategy is from the particular venture should anything change or happen that is unexpected. They will want this documented and usually want more than one exit from the venture should they need it. We spoke about the importance of exits earlier, and a sophisticated JV partner will certainly want to know about this and how you have factored it in.

Competence and reliability

A potential partner wants to be able to see that you can and have done property investment successfully. Providing examples of property deals you have previously sourced for yourself or others, or showing what you could do with current property opportunities available, shows someone that you are competent in investing in property. Having referrals or testimonials from previous partners or individuals who know of your work in the property world, can also build someone's trust in you. A potential partner wants to know that their money is secure and that you will use it to its full potential.

Security

Private investors will want to know that you can provide them with financial security at the beginning of the partnership, and let them know exactly where their money will stand in the property investment. I always try to put myself in the shoes of the investor and think "how can I reduce their risk and increase their security?" This is absolutely vital.

Different investors will want different levels of security in a particular venture. Explaining the security you can offer to an investor will build credibility and trust early on. This will mean that the investor will know where they stand and can voice any concerns or discuss changes they want to make. This will highlight the agreement for both this property investment opportunity and others in the future.

There will be different ways this can be done, such as having the property in joint names or under the name of the investor. I would always recommend seeking legal advice to make sure all points are considered and covered off legally to ensure security.

Reassure their concerns and make sure it is a win/win

Make sure that the investor has no concerns, as you are looking to build an on-going relationship with them. Alleviating any concerns they may have about the property investment from day one ensures them that their money is in safe hands. Ask them if they have any worries or something they are concerned about with the investment. This allows them to also feel involved with the practicalities of the property deal. Being able to answer or solve any issues that your partner has, gives them a better understanding about the world of property investment, and provides trust and security.

If you have found a property and have some great ideas on how to add value as above, done all your due diligence, and you need a cash-rich investor, JV's can be a fantastic way to help finance your deals, especially in the current economic climate. You will ultimately need to build rapport with different investors to see how you can work with them long term.

Case study number 2: A Joint venture of my own.

After starting out in property and then beginning to source properties for others I found that I had built some close relationships with certain clients who then became Joint venture partners. It definitely taught me a valuable lesson which was to never assume anything about anyone or their financial position, as this particular person had a lot more money to invest than I first thought.

So how did the Joint venture work?

Well as explained earlier there are many different ways joint ventures can work and it is very important that when they are undertaken, both parties sit down and agree in detail a solid plan moving forward. After getting to know my partner well and getting to know their his goals and what was important to him, (as discussed earlier this is vitally important) I realised that he was more concerned with capital growth in the future and saw property as at least a ten to fifteen year plan. This was because he already had another form of income which was his main source, and property investing was an addition. Whilst I am still in property for the long term, I was also in a position where I needed the cash flow more urgently as I was going full time into property. This proved to work well and our agreement stated that I would receive more of the cash flow and he would receive more of the capital growth long term. We then had an agreement that this could be reviewed in the future, and if both parties agreed we may decide to change the agreement to a 50/50 arrangement.

This Joint venture has proved to work well and I believe this is because of the concrete relationship formed between us. This can take time but I have found this to cause the least confusion or problems later down the line. Now with any agreement I believe you should definitely get legal advice and have a watertight agreement, however I have personally found that it is vitally important to spend time with potential partners from the outset and get to know their long term goals. This is because although the agreement is legally documented, you want to try to avoid any issues longer term which could result in heartache and more legal costs.

I often get people that are new to property say things such as 'well I have only just started and have only bought my first property so why would anyone want to work with me at the moment'. Now there is a famous quote from Henry Ford which is 'Whether you think you can, or you think you can't, you're right'.

Therefore by thinking you can't you will give off the negative impression that will likely result in not attracting any partners. I have to admit that these thoughts crossed my mind at the start but then this particular venture changed my view completely. This was because this partner never actually asked how many properties I owned myself. This was very interesting and made me realise that this was not a barrier at all. They said that they were impressed with my knowledge of the area, and how I had thought through the proposal in great detail to present not only a good investment proposition but also different ways to exit if needed, therefore minimising the risk. This was a real mind shift and accelerated my development. Now don't get me wrong if you have bought property before then using it as social proof is a good thing to do, and certain people may demand this. But if you haven't then don't let this be a barrier to not progressing at all. You can still research your area and find attractive investments, meaning that there will still be people who are willing to invest in you.

JV Disclaimer: In 2013 the FCA brought in a report highlighting the protocol regarding Joint Ventures and non-regulated investment schemes. For more information refer to the link below.

Link: https://www.fca.org.uk/static/documents/policy-statements/ps13-03.pdf

Summary: There are many different strategies available to use in property, meaning that you do not have to rely on one income stream or way of making money from property investment. It is important to pick the one that you feel is right for you, and fits well with your circumstances and tools available, at that time. Timing is very important.

10. PROPERTY IS A NUMBERS GAME

Making money from property and building a profitable property portfolio is a numbers game, when broken down to its basic form. Numbers may be your strong point so if they are you are in luck and can get excited. If numbers and analysis are not your strong point then you will benefit strongly from learning this. When I first started I found that I enjoyed running the numbers on properties in my head and on my calculator, but I found out that this was not enough to get systemised to the highest level. (There is more on systems later in the chapter)

I soon realised that I had to learn the skill of thinking in numbers if I was going to make money from property investing.

> Important note: Viewing property numerically (as opposed to emotionally) makes a lot of money. Emotion can lose a lot of money.

The first skill in numbers is knowing exactly where you are now.

Viewing numbers when starting out in property

I often hear people say something like 'I have tried looking for properties and there just aren't any suitable deals out there for me'. An old mentor of mine often said that the devil is always in the detail. That taught me to delve deeper into situations to find out more of the detail to make a conclusion.

So when this has been said in the past I have then asked how many viewings they are doing weekly and monthly and usually get a response like ' well I viewed five the other day and they all went at asking price and some even above.' This is a typical response and this is where playing the numbers is so vital.

No matter what some people say, even the most experienced investors will have times when they view properties which are not suitable or the seller or agent just gets a higher offer. It happens, and the key is to accept this and move on, and not give up. (The importance of never giving up is discussed in another section).

Experienced, seasoned investors have a system in place. That means they do regular viewings and play the numbers game, as this increases their odds of success, and allows them to track performance as well.

That is the beauty of numbers: they don't judge and they don't lie.

So when you are starting out, the key is to throw as many darts against the board as you can in a strategic, planned way. Planning your strategy and area is vital and this is mentioned earlier in the book, so once you have done this it is key to get your viewing numbers up. Now there are many benefits to this including building long lasting solid relationships with agents which will likely prove very fruitful over the years for you. But as well as that you will be able to get a real-time idea of the amount of viewings you need to do to achieve your goals.

Now property investing is like any other business or walk of life in that the more you do it, the slicker and more polished you will become. I am sure when Roger Federer first picked up a tennis racquet he wasn't immediately the unbelievable tennis player that he became. I am sure it took years and years of practice, repetition, testing and perfecting his craft to achieve that.

You should look at investing in property no differently - if you are serious of course. Remember: treat property as a business from day 1.

So you start out and let's say you initially view 50 properties over a period of time. Now it's important to say here that there were a lot of properties that I viewed when I started that I wouldn't ever touch again with a bargepole, like low cash-flowing property and I also got emotionally attached and overpaid for a property. Hopefully, with this book, I have connected with you before you have started, so you won't make the same mistakes that I did. If not, then don't worry we are always learning and improving along the way. Even years down the line you will be testing and tweaking to find new ways of improving what you are doing.

When you initially view the first 50 properties you will find that some will fit your strategy and work, and some will not because, even if they do work at a certain figure, the vendor may not be willing to accept that figure. The key here is to not panic, just systematically go through each property one by one to assess them. If the property just does not work then you can put it to the back of the pile. You can then cherry pick the main contenders from the 50 that you have viewed. It is important to clarify the profile of the types of properties that you feel are ones you can offer on. This means that when you view the next 50 properties you will not arrange to view ones that don't fit that profile.

When you start out and view 50 properties, then if 10 are good investment propositions you will be doing well. From that ten you could offer on all and then if you can strike deals on 2 or 3 then you will have a good conversion rate. As I became more experienced in property I have found that for every 50 I viewed, half of them, or even over half, may be suitable investment properties. This is because my knowledge had increased but I had also built solid agent relationships and they knew what I was looking for. That meant I began to only view ones that would fit a strict criteria and fit my rules, which we know is key.

This is where the numbers come into their own as you can test and track. If it takes 50 properties to agree two sales, then you will know that if you want to buy 4 that month, you will need to increase your viewing numbers. This process is key and something that I found really helped me to systemise my business and see what was actually happening. Another advantage of working in this way is it allows you to put the associated costs against this, and work out the true profitability of your business.

Your numbers with your property purchases

The same rules will then apply with properties that you buy and add into your portfolio. By getting into the habit of using numbers as your guide, you are in a much better position to make informed decisions about this as well.

The key with property investing as with any business is to spend your time on things that generate income. The less time you spend on things that don't generate you money, and the more time you spend on things that do, based on your numbers, this will be directly proportionate to the amount of money you make from property.

Spreadsheets, statistics, data and things such as this did not come naturally to me when I started buying property. I believe this is an important point as often we have strengths in, and enjoy, certain parts of the process more than others. I enjoyed the sourcing of the property, the negotiation, the relationship building which seemed to come more naturally to me as I had been exposed to these areas in previous jobs before. I had to learn to embrace the statistics and data side, to make sure this was all in order and up to speed. One of the key things that I learnt was that by doing this and focusing on the numbers you can actually highlight where you are making money, which is very exciting. You can then do more of this particular thing to make more money, which is even more exciting.

Now some people will be reading this and thinking that getting excited about the numbers is like watching paint drying but I have found that there are certain skills needed in every walk of life and property is the same. If you want to drive a car you have to pass your theory test and learn to do this. The numbers are key as you need to know what you are doing to be able to improve it. If you do not know what you are doing then you can't improve it.

The most successful property investors and businesses are not there by accident and most of them have not had a silver spoon or a head start through their upbringing. Once they have based their strategies around those who are already successful, they can then test and continually improve. It is that final 10% that often makes the difference to your success and bottom line.

Your use of time with evidence from the numbers is key. It all comes back to spending the majority of your time on things that generate income. If the numbers show that one particular strategy makes the most profit, then you should be spending more time on this, and this will directly boost your income accordingly.

Sounds simple but many people often miss this.

Summary: Using the numbers as your benchmark is key to tracking your progress. If you spend your time in the most productive way, based on the information your numbers give, then you will be well on your way to achieving the success you desire.

11. WHY BUILDING YOUR PROPERTY POWER TEAM IS SO IMPORTANT

A vital part of your property success will be building a power team around you that you can trust and rely on. Your property power team is made up of the professionals that you use in the day to day running of your business. Successful business people know that they cannot do everything on their own, so they hire people who are great at the things that they are not so good at, or are not qualified to do. A great power team not only ensures the smooth running of your business, but also has the potential to provide you with referral commissions, amongst other opportunities. The different parties will likely agree to this as you are helping them grow their business as well. All the members of the power team are equally important to your success.

This is often what a lot of people forget. A lot of people in small businesses or those who are new to property have the 'I'm the only one who can do it' mentality. They believe that *'if I don't do it, no one's going to do it, and no one can do it as good as me.'* Now unless you are qualified in everything then you cannot do all the parts needed in the property buying process anyway, such as the legal aspects, or arranging the mortgage finance. However, many people will try to do all the parts they believe they can do such as renovating a house themselves, and this can often take a lot longer and cost a lot more in the long run.

So who is needed in your property power team?

You will likely use a number of different people in your power team, depending on your own property strategy.

Here are some of the key ones I use:

Letting agents – if you need to let a property, you will need a letting agent. You can also try to let the property yourself but you then may not end up being a property investor or the entrepreneur you set out to be, you will end up being a letting agent. Now that is great if that is what you want to do. Do you have experience in that area, and is doing this of particular interest to you? If the answer is "Yes" then that's fine but it is all down to your individual strategy and what you want out of property investment. Most people get into property investment to buy and profit from property, but end up trying to do too many things as they think it is saving money.

By using a letting agent they will be valuable in many ways: firstly you're letting agent will be able to help you evaluate properties that you purchase. You can also speak to your letting agent beforehand to look at what the market rental is for the properties that are of interest to you. This will help you greatly when doing your due diligence on a property and working out the potential rental return. Now you may be thinking that you are not sure what to say to letting agents initially, or questioning whether they will take you seriously if you have not already let a property with them. Don't worry – there are many questions I can share with you that I ask new letting agents to build rapport and trust.

Firstly I ask their overall view of the rental market to build this rapport, and this also shows that I see them as a person of influence, and respect their opinion.

I then ask them things such as:

1. Where do you find that you rent properties quickly and easily with competitive rents?
2. Which areas do you struggle to let properties and why?
3. If someone was to give you a deposit for a property where would you buy and why?

I do this often in my business and I have preferred letting agents that I use and go to for this information. Now these are just initial questions to ask and you will find the agents you can work with well as you go along. Remember if you ask them where is good to rent and they just mention the roads they have properties available, then be wary as this might not be the case.

The more letting agents you can work with and leverage, the better. You will be able to find agents who are specialists in different tenant types such as DSS (also known as LHA 'local housing allowance' or council paid rent), working professionals or students. The more you know then the more options you will have in building your portfolio. It will also be of value if you decide to buy properties for other clients which is another strategy we have discussed in the book.

Remember, your relationship with your letting agent is

crucial in ensuring you get good tenants. Good tenants mean bills get paid on time and your property is looked after. Bad tenants can mean late payments and this is something you want to avoid.

As we can see a letting agent is a key part of your team. Sometimes new investors or landlords start out using a letting agent and once they have built a sizeable portfolio then they take it in-house. This is an option, but those that do this need to make sure they are up to date with all legislative changes at all times. You will need to define where your interests lie and where you feel your time is best spent.

Property solicitor / conveyancer – a capable property solicitor will ensure the smooth handling of your property transactions. This is essential to make sure the properties complete in the timescale required to ensure a smooth transition. When I first got into property I quickly realised the importance of the legal work completing on time, and how if one part of the chain is slow it can affect timescales on other parts of the buying process. Now sometimes there are unforeseen circumstances that cannot be helped, but you want to make sure you find a solicitor who is proactive and works to resolve any issues or problems as quickly as possible. If this part of the process is slow it can affect other things such as the tradesmen, as if they are booked in for a certain time and it doesn't complete on time then they may have to go to another job, which could cause delays.

Property investment coach – many successful property

investors are now deciding to add a property mentor to their team to multiply their results and keep their property business on the right track. This can be of great use, as you can model someone who has achieved the results you are looking for.

Property accountant – an accountant experienced in the field of property will make sure that you can keep as much of your hard-earned profit as possible. As with all parts of your property business, it is important to start as you mean to go on. Many people start out buying property and then speak to an accountant further down the line. It is often a lot easier to speak to an accountant from day 1 before you start buying. This is because they will not only do your tax returns for you and keep you compliant, but they will also make sure that you are claiming everything you can do legally as well. They should be able to sit down with you at the start and work out the best tax strategy for you long term, as you can inform them of your future plans and goals. You may be buying for your children or want to set up a limited company, and they can advise on the best route for you to take. This is a vitally important part of your investment plan.

Mortgage broker – a specialist investment mortgage broker will search the ever-changing finance market for the best products to fund your deals, and fight your corner if things go wrong such as a property being down-valued by a surveyor. We like to use brokers who have access to all of the financial products on the market to ensure we can get the best deals for ourselves and clients.

Bridging finance company – if you are doing short term development projects or creative finance deals then a good Bridger will be indispensable. This will allow you to fund projects that you may wish to sell on for a profit.

Furnishings company – if you are in the buy-to-let market then a responsive property furnishings company will be very useful to you for when you do furnished lets. If you are buying furnishing in bulk then you should be able to work out a favourable rate.

Investment property insurance broker – when you're insuring a rental property a good insurance broker should be able to source the best product for the purpose. If you put multiple properties through one insurance company they should be able to give you a multiple property landlord rate.

Tradesmen – Finding reliable tradesmen will be essential to you when you are looking to build your portfolio. You will often need tradesmen for buying and selling property, or when buying and renting property. As mentioned earlier, refurbishing property is a great way to add value to a property and for this you will need reliable, honest tradesmen who complete work in a timely manner. When looking to build a portfolio you will want to know as many good builders as possible. Like other fields, good people are often busy and tradesmen are no different. Sometimes people make the mistake of thinking that they can take months and months to complete on a property, and then the builder they want to use will wait around for them. This unfortunately can leave you disappointed as they will have other jobs to go to. Once you have found good builders and tradesmen then it is important to keep them updated on your progress when buying property so that you can book them in and give them plenty of notice. Like everything we do in property investment we are looking for long-term relationships. By acting in this way they will want to work with you long term as it will benefit you both.

Below are some points to consider when finding good reliable tradesmen:

1. Get a fixed price for a Job- Not a day rate!
2. Ensure they invest themselves or at least deal with other property investors.
3. Ensure they have a good knowledge of the market
4. Don't just go with the lowest price
5. Do your research and ask for referrals

I have been fortunate to find good tradesmen in my time in property and it makes life a lot easier let me tell you. The relationship has then grown to the point where you may do more creative things on properties where you buy and then sell. For example in the past I have worked closely with certain builders where I have included them in the back end profit of the project. Therefore instead of paying them their usual rate, you pay them a reduced rate for the job and then include them on the profits of the sale. It may be that they are just on a percentage of the sale profit and do not take a weekly wage at all for the job. I remember doing this with a builder who is now a good friend of mine. We had been working together for a while and I approached him with a proposition. I was buying a property to 'flip' (sell) and wanted to keep upfront costs as low as possible as I am sure you can appreciate. Therefore I offered him 25% of the profits on the job, in exchange for him not taking a wage for doing the work. I paid for the materials for the job but there were no weekly wages involved. When the property was sold he got 25% of the profits which proved to be in the region of £5000. He was overjoyed as that was more than he would have been paid for the 4-week refurbishment, and I was happy as I didn't have to find as much money upfront. This has turned into a very solid relationship and he is now a key member of my team and actually became a sourcing client as well! This can be a win/win for both parties as they can end up making more money in total, and you do not have to find as much money upfront therefore helping cash flow. This would likely be something that you do with someone you have built a long-term solid relationship with, but it is just an example to highlight the future possibilities when you have a trusted team of tradesmen around you.

> Important tip: The sooner you realise that you cannot do everything yourself the better. There is a saying 'Your network is your net worth and it is very true'.

As you can see a power team is vitally important to not only allow you to run your business smoothly, but it can also help to promote your business as well and lead to a referral network.

Summary: Building relationships is of paramount importance and is the key to results and success. It is a fact that we cannot do everything ourselves and we need other people in all areas so that we can build a successful portfolio. If you build strong relationships with others then they will go to great lengths to help you achieve your goals. That is true leverage.

12. SURROUND YOURSELF WITH LIKE-MINDED PEOPLE

This one thing managed to accelerate my success in property tenfold. For years I thought about property and even mentioned it at previous jobs only to be told that it was for other people, and you needed endless pots of capital to invest. When I made a decision to get myself educated in property and surround myself with like-minded people, it became clear that this was not necessarily the case. The positive energy I got from surrounding myself with others on the same journey was priceless and a real contributor to my success.

'Jim Rohn states that you are the average of the 5 people you spend the most time with' and so it is vital to surround yourself with the right people for you.

I remember how lonely it felt on June 12th 2009 at 4.02pm. I had just finished my last shift at what I planned to be the last Job I would ever have in my life. The clock turned 4pm and as I walked out the doors it dawned on me that I would be doing that for the last time. After a slightly heavy weekend to celebrate that I had achieved my initial goal of going into property full time, I remember waking up on the Monday morning and the reality kicked in even more.

There I was in my front room and whilst I was excited and focused on what I was doing next, I also will freely admit that initially I felt alone and isolated from my previous environment. I do however recall at this point forcing myself to think about two statements which I had heard from previous successful entrepreneurs and they were:

1. As an entrepreneur if it's not a bit uncomfortable then you may not be challenging yourself enough
2. Surround yourself with like-minded people at every possible occasion.

These sayings really hit home and motivated me in a huge way, and if you find yourself in this position then hopefully they will do the same for you as well.

I kept thinking to myself that if it was easy then everyone would be doing it, and I kept repeating this to myself and telling myself that it was only a short term thing. After feeling this way for a period of time I then began to ask myself the question, how can I surround myself with the right kind of people who are like-minded and following the same path? I refused to believe I was the only one in this position in my local area and knew there must be others feeling the same.

So I began to research local property events to go to, and attended other events as well, such as local landlord forums and business events. I made this a really significant part of my weekly schedule and was then fortunate after a period of time to meet a fellow property investor also from the West Midlands, Jackie Goodman, who I really clicked with immediately which felt fantastic, and suddenly I was not feeling as alone as I did. We talked and chatted about our goals and where we wanted to take our property careers and we both realised the importance of being around like-minded people regularly. It was at this point we decided to start our own local networking event, aimed at supporting people in this very situation.

So how did this meet affect my situation?

The decision to start this property meet I have to say was a real factor in my property journey, and to my success in general over the coming years, as it was for Jackie who has also been very successful. Jackie and I continue to work together in property to this day.

Starting the meeting was a really rewarding experience as it provided a supportive environment for not only myself and Jackie, but the other people who started to attend as well. It was only a small informal meet to start with, and I remember our first meeting when we only had a handful of people attend. This continued for a few months but we kept going and were persistent which is so important to do, and we started to get the word out there more and more after a period of time. Starting the meet and then growing it to a decent sized group was really valuable to everybody who attended, and we ended up moving from a small room at a local pub to a bigger room in a sports and health club.

Through this meeting I met so many inspirational people and contacts who I still see many of today and as time went on I realised that I was not isolated, and there were so many positive, driven people out there who all wanted the same thing as me. This feeling was fantastic and I began to see regular people weekly rather than just the once a month at the meet. We were also able to attract great speakers, who were able to share their knowledge and experiences as well, helping the group even further.

> Important note: We do not know when or how we will meet the right people for us. If we put ourselves in the right places such as networking events, we give ourselves the best chance of meeting like-minded, driven individuals to associate with, which is what we all need in abundance.

I cannot stress the value enough of regular networking and I would always suggest that someone starts their own group if they can as well. I found it a fantastic way to meet others. Even if it is only a small group initially then the knowledge, experience and support you can give each other is vital, and it should be a real contributor to your success. Unfortunately if you don't surround yourself with supportive people you can get dragged down by other people who are often ignorant and will always see the negative side. Don't let this happen to you, as you can succeed with the right people around you!

Summary: Surrounding yourself with like-minded people is key. It is so important to keep positive energy around you with members of your power team and with the other people you spend your day-to-day time with. Being around negative people can be really damaging and put doubts in your mind that do not need to be there. If you wanted to be a great footballer then it is a good idea to spend the majority of your time around other great footballers. The same applies to property investment.

13. ALWAYS ACT WITH INTEGRITY AND HONESTY AND AIM FOR A WIN/WIN SOLUTION

Throughout my years in property and business I have always aimed for a win/win solution and always acted with integrity and honesty. I pride myself on these traits and only associate myself with people who feel the same about this as I do.

Property investing will put you in many different situations with different people, depending on the strategies that you use. I have found in my business that it is not only about being ethical with sellers, but with my clients as well, making sure it is a win/win situation.

Being ethical with property sellers

To begin with, when dealing with someone who is selling a property, it is vitally important to build rapport and trust with the seller. It is no good charging in like a bull in a china shop, saying that you will only offer them a certain amount for their property.

When looking at property and making offers it will likely be in one of two ways, which will be dealing with an estate agent or directly with a private vendor. Now the situations are often totally different and this is something that I teach my students today with the people I mentor. The essence of a win/win situation and good ethics however should always be employed in both situations.

The first thing I do when dealing with a private seller is assure them that they are dealing with someone professional, and I always assure them that the conversations will be confidential. You will need to put yourself in the seller's shoes and try to understand how they feel. It can be a very distressing time and they will be looking for a solution to their problem, and often very quickly. This is where you come in and I am always asking myself how I can help someone solve their problem. The way to do this is to ask them what they want, and what is most important to them. It is only then that you can find out if you can help, and give them what they need.

Don't mess a seller or agent around

What is extremely important is not messing a seller or agent around. It can be very stressful for someone trying to sell their property, and even worse if they have to do it by a certain time. It is really important that you don't give a vendor or agent false hope. Don't tell them that you can purchase their property if you have no intention of doing so. If you can't help them, then be upfront and let them know so they can find another buyer. This is very important and it is vital that you are quick and decisive.

Communication is also really important. This can often be the key to making the vendor feel comfortable and at ease, meaning in return you are more likely to complete the purchase with them. Keep them updated throughout the process to show them you are acting efficiently on their behalf.

I have experienced both sides of the coin so understand the importance of this. I remember once at the start of my career when I lost communication with a private vendor and it cost me dearly. Unfortunately I learnt the hard way, and ended up losing the purchase. It was actually at the start back in 2008 and I remember going to see a private vendor who was looking to sell their property. After viewing the property, I agreed with them that I would purchase the property. I then said that I would call them later on and update them with news on the purchase. What I meant by this was that I would call them when I had some news but the seller thought I meant later on that day. As I didn't have any news until the following week I decided that I would call them the following week. Because the seller of the property thought I meant later that day, when I didn't call they thought that I didn't want to proceed and ended up agreeing another sale. The poor communication on this particular deal cost me many thousands of pounds and it is a mistake I would not make again. Therefore communication is key so you don't make the same mistake as I did even once! The key is to find out the expectations of the seller and how often they want to be kept updated, and then keep the rapport going from here.

Being ethical, being nice and trustworthy, has paid off for me in the past on a number of occasions. One of the times that comes to mind is when working with estate agents, and the fact that they have then remembered me when properties come to market that they think fit my criteria. Being ethical and honest in my approach means that they have then wanted to work with me, rather than other people who they think have the wrong motives, or will mess their sellers around.

Is everybody ethical?

Unfortunately as with any walk of life there are people out there who are not ethical and unfortunately people can be taken in by them at times. There has been a lot of negative media coverage in the past regarding investment companies who were apparently taking advantage of desperate sellers. Because of this negative press, some sellers and those closest to them, can be sceptical of your motives. This happened to me a few years ago now when I went to see a private seller at their home. Now this particular seller had actually had some other companies and individuals contact them beforehand and had said that they had been offended by some of the offers they had, and had felt that they were being taken advantage of. It took me time to build rapport and trust with them and actually assure them that I wasn't of this vein and that I was ethical. I always try to make a point of visiting every potential seller if I can (another advantage of the area being local) even if at first I do not think that it will be a property I could purchase, based on the information I have been given over the phone. This is because it gives me chance to find out more information and really get to know their situation and if I can help. I also believe in karma as well and think that even if I cannot help them myself, I may be able to put them in contact with someone who can. This actually happened with this particular seller, as I found out that what I could offer them would not be enough due to their debts and situation. I mentioned to them that I knew an estate agent who may be able to help and that I would happily get them to contact them if they wish. They were open to this idea, giving the agent a chance to sell their property. I was then pleased to find out that they subsequently did sell the property for the amount the seller needed to move forward. This made me feel good that I was able to help them, and although I did not benefit financially, it was nice to help them and I believe that it is important to help others as what goes around comes around.

Being ethical with your clients

Your clients in truth can be your best supporters and your best sales force when you treat them well. On the other hand it only takes one client to have one bad experience for them to lose trust in you completely. This in turn means that because of their experience they will certainly not refer you to anyone else. In Joe Girrard's book *'The World's Greatest Salesman'* he talks about The Law of 250, where he says the average person touches at least 250 people in their life. Based on this it is clear to see how disastrous treating someone unfairly could be. Now this is not to say that challenges will not arise at times, but it is always important to be upfront and work with people to make sure that their experiences are positive, and you are aiming for a win/win.

This has always been very important to me and has actually been a great driver for my business when working with clients. For example I really found this to be of benefit when working with one of my first clients. For the purpose of this example we'll call him Ben. Now I first met Ben at a property event and subsequently met up after this event to discuss his requirements and what he was looking for from his property investments. Now Ben by his own admission was slightly sceptical and nervous about working with someone else. He had been introduced to some other people sourcing property in the past and felt that they had just been trying to sell him any old property so they could profit. Over the next few meetings I built really good rapport with Ben and really got to know his goals in property and life. I found out that he wanted to invest so that he had assets that would cash flow and then appreciate so he had money to pay for his children's university fees in years to come. From his own words not mine, he was impressed that I was taking the time to actually get to know his situation, and find out what was most important to him on a short term and a long-term basis. I was also able to help Ben with the letting of his property by contacting the local council with whom I already had an existing relationship. This made the whole process smoother and more efficient for him which he was grateful for. I am still in contact with Ben and he assures me that his property purchases have already helped with his children's university fund which is fantastic to hear.

From doing this and aiming for a win/win situation this relationship has proved invaluable. I have been able to help Ben invest in property and profit for many years, and in return he has referred me to other people which has helped me grow my business as well.

The importance of ethics and a win/win scenario is something I always have employed, and will continue to employ, and is now something I also stress with my team in my business.

The different laws of influence in relation to working with others

Many people often forget the powers of the laws of reciprocity, likeability, authority, and other laws of influence. There are many of these laws and they can really help aid you on your journey.

What is the law of reciprocity?

The law of reciprocity states that in order to receive something, you must first give something.

This is something that a lot of people know and understand but they do not use these laws. If you want to buy a profitable property and build trust with a vendor which is essential, then first of all you must give something to them. A lot of the time that can be a no obligation discussion and valuation of their property, or an online report through your website. Whatever it is, it is there to provide trust and build rapport with the vendor.

The law of likeability

The law of likeability is also a hugely important law of influence, as no one ever buys from someone they do not like. People don't generally spend time with people they don't like, and no-one does anything they don't like, unless they are forced to.

In order to get win-win, empowering situations with people you must be a likeable person, and it is vitally important not to underestimate the importance of this throughout your property and business career.

The law of authority

The law of authority is also very important in different situations. People who have authority can do great things. You need to be viewed as a leader not a follower. You want to be viewed as someone who has authority, positioning and charisma. You need to project your knowledge and power as people will then trust your opinion. As I have mentioned before people tend to follow rather than lead, and they tend to be told what to do by various people or organisations/media. If you can project authority, and are likeable, then you will direct many more people to outcomes that work both for them and you, and therefore achieve a win/win.

Summary: Being ethical in all situations is very important to me, and I would recommend that everyone does the same. It is possible to be ethical and get win/win situations for both parties. Do not underestimate the laws of likeability and reciprocity as these are also very important when working with others.

14. LEARNING FROM SOMEONE WHO HAS BEEN THERE AND DONE IT IS KEY – FIND A GOOD MENTOR

Having the right guidance and advice is crucial to your property investment success and similarly to other fields you often need a good mentor. If you are looking to kick start your own multi-million pound property portfolio then you want to find someone who can advise you on all the mistakes to avoid along the way.

When I was at university I had a tutor to help me along my way and when I started out in property I realised this was just as vital for my success. At university I needed someone to help me learn the modules and topics, and property investing is no different.

By avoiding these common expensive mistakes you will be able to set clear and achievable goals and come up with a strategy which encourages you to stick to one plan.

Having someone to guide and support you through building your own property investment portfolio will provide you with the motivation you need to get started. For these reasons your property mentor must be the real deal and have successfully invested in property themselves.

Here are some key tips to look out for when choosing your property investment mentor:

- Make sure they listen before giving you any advice - the support and guidance need to be tailored to what you want to personally gain from property investment, each investor is different.

- Make sure you are able to set out a clear plan and strategy before you start.

- Make sure they are the real deal! If you want the right advice, and to avoid any costly mistakes, your mentor must have experienced the field first-hand themselves, or their advice may not be very useful. Ask for referrals and to speak to previous people they have mentored for a testimonial.

- Avoid those who immediately ask for a payment - A one to one chat regarding your investment goals and your financial situation should initially be free to make sure you are in a position to discuss your property investment options.

- Make sure you can contact them - A great property investment can appear at any time and you want the right sound advice when this does happen; you should be able to get hold of your mentor when you need them most. The whole point of a mentorship, especially a year-long program, is that you have the support through the day to day and weekly or monthly issues that arise.

- You want honest advice – If they are able to share their own honest experiences and mistakes during property investment it is sign that you can trust their advice.

- Go with your gut instincts – your instincts are there for a reason. Do you get a good feel about the particular person or company, do you think they are trustworthy and reliable?

- Make sure you set realistic goals and are made accountable. There is no use setting unrealistic goals and similarly there is no use in someone telling you that you are doing well when you are being lazy.

By following these tips you should put yourself in a fantastic position to find the right mentor for yourself long term, which ultimately will give you the best chance of success, and fast track your achievements. A mentor will not only give you all the tools you need, but he/she is someone to confide in and someone who can support you in moments of doubt.

> Important note: Having someone there to help you in times of need is vital, and certainly was for me. It may only be an answer to a question, or a bit of moral support when making a tough decision, but it makes you feel part of a team, and that you have a support network around of people who have your best interests at heart. Remember if they have walked the walk they will have been there and come through the other side.

I remember sitting down in 2008 when I was looking to choose a mentor. I had been to property seminars and other events, and really saw the benefit of finding a mentor, as I felt I needed someone there who could guide me in the right direction. I had however heard some horror stories of people who had paid thousands to be mentored and not really got the support they needed. After being on one particular event for a weekend, I really clicked with someone who I subsequently decided to be mentored by. This was a huge step for me both financially and emotionally, as I knew that things were getting serious and I really had to make property work for me. I decided to take the leap of faith, and this is something that many successful people I have met in property talk about. They usually highlight the fact that they were often unsure at times, and scared as it was unknown ground, but they made the brave decision to take the leap of faith and pursue their goals. I was certainly no different, and it is why I took my time in finding the right mentor. The right mentor might not always be the most well-known person, or the person with the biggest reputation. It is important that they are right for you as an individual, and by following the rules above as a guideline you should be able to find someone who is right for you long term. I personally clicked with the mentor I had because they understood the fact that I wanted to learn the basics of property first before moving onto other strategies. I remember saying to them on my first day, "It feels really boring to say this with all the creative strategies out there, but I just want to learn about buy to let first and start with small 2-bed terraced houses." Their response was, "Pete it is definitely not boring, it is the foundation of a solid long term business which will serve you well in years to come." I still remember that conversation today and am truly grateful I received this advice. It also made me realise that this particular mentor understood what I wanted to achieve first before moving on.

Summary: Successful people learn from successful people before them. Learning from someone who has been there and done it is vital. Their knowledge and experience will help you greatly, and mean that you can shortcut your route to success.

15. SET REALISTIC BUT CHALLENGING GOALS

One of the biggest things I have seen stifle many people's success is the goals that they set themselves from the outset. It has been the case in the past that I have seen many people make progress with their property career, however because their goals have been unrealistic it has meant that they feel they have not achieved what they would like to, which in turn has de-motivated them.

This actually happened to me after my first couple of years in property. I began to immerse myself in the property world, which was fantastic, but it also meant that I had exposure to many others that I felt were making more progress than me.

The fact of the matter is that each situation is different. Every individual's life is different in terms of the time they have available, the knowledge they currently have, and the money they have available to invest. So the key is to certainly set goals which are realistic for you to achieve.

Being an ambitious person you can probably imagine some of the goals I had at the start for myself. I wanted to be earning hundreds of thousands from property investing, and have a multi-million pound portfolio straight away. This however was not a realistic target when I first started. I was working full-time in a job and this was not the only issue. I was just starting out so I had lots to learn and also had limited funds available as well. I had to focus myself and start with an initial target that was realistic. I decided that I would go full time in property once I had achieved 60-70% of what my current salary was. This was still going to be a challenging goal, but I felt it was realistic with the resources I currently had available. I felt that by getting to 60-70% of my current salary, I could live on this although it would be a bit of a struggle.

So I began to build my strategy around this which I felt was extremely important. This is something I cannot stress enough, which is reaching your first target before moving on. Too often, I have seen people who are new to property take on things which are just too far-reaching for them at that point. It is great to dream big and we all should, but it is also vitally important to be realistic about how you can make positive strides forward. It is then vital to reward yourself when you do, so that you feel empowered by the fact that you have achieved a milestone and are moving in the right direction.

> Important note: Rewarding yourself at milestones is vital, as it trains your mind to realise that when you get to a focal point there are good things that await. This will then keep you focused to work hard to achieve each milestone.

Let me give you an example from when I started. It was 2010 and I had been investing for a couple of years at this point, and had built up a portfolio I was proud of, and that gave me a solid passive income each month. I felt like I was then ready to set another goal and move forward with my business. So I began to research other strategies in property which I felt could provide me with another income stream and diversify my business. This could only happen because I had bought back my time by not having to work full time in my job as well. I went on to research other strategies such as deal packaging and attracting joint venture finance and this was going to take time to research, learn and build. If I had tried to do this while I was working full time as well as building my own portfolio, then it would likely have been just too much, and led to frustration and overwhelm, and not being productive. This was because to start sourcing for others as well, was going to multiply the amount of time I needed to spend on the business to do it well. I didn't have that extra time then as I was working full time and my spare time was spent on viewing properties for myself and building my own portfolio. Unfortunately I see this at times with different people, and it can be soul destroying as they do not feel like they have made the progress they want to. The truth is that often they have made great strides forward, more than many, but the goals they set were not realistic based on their circumstances at the time. It is not they can't do it in time, but to try and do it all in one go does not work. Don't put yourself in this position, as you do not want to be de-motivated by feeling like you have not made progress.

Summary: Set challenging goals but be realistic. You do not want to de-motivate yourself and become overwhelmed. This can be disastrous for your long term progress. Look at your current situation and the resources you have available, including finances and time. From here you can make a plan to achieve your first goal, which should then allow you to achieve many more in the future.

16. EXPECT UPS AND DOWNS ALONG THE WAY

As sure as the day is long, there will be ups and downs along your journey. Property investing is no different and is like any other business or life path in that sense. I wouldn't believe anyone who tells you any different. The key here is to aim to minimise the amount of downs you get along the way and when you do, to find an objective way of dealing with them.

So how can we minimise the down times?

Unfortunately there isn't a way to completely eradicate them as life and property can throw up unexpected challenges along the way. The first way to minimise this though is to plan your strategy out from the outset as we have discussed earlier in the book.

How to deal with challenges when they do arise

When you do get problems and hurdles to overcome in your property journey, I have always found it crucial to have a supportive network around me, who I can bounce ideas off to get a different perspective on the situation. This is vitally important as getting a different perspective can often shine a different light, and allow you to work through this so that it will not happen again. You will probably have heard the saying in life that a 'problem shared is a problem halved' and this is also true in property.

The important thing is to take many of the steps highlighted in this book to make sure that you minimise risk and hopefully there will be very few hurdles for you to overcome along the journey.

If challenges do occur, then I always follow the same process which is:

1. Identify the problem.
2. Aim to identify the cause of the problem to eradicate this.
3. Look at the options I now have to overcome this.

By following this same pattern you will be able to make positive strides forward if problems do occur, and not let them affect your journey on the whole.

Summary: Expect ups and downs along your journey. This is something that happens in all walks of life and property investing is no different. It is important to enjoy the ups that you get and reward yourself, and then look at the downs as an opportunity to learn more to make them less likely to happen again. If you follow the blueprint above, you should be able overcome any challenges or problems that arise which will ultimately make you stronger in the long term.

17. PERSISTENCE IS KEY

Being persistent throughout your journey in property is absolutely vital to your success. I was always told when I was younger that 'nothing comes easy' and 'anything worth having is worth working for'. This is true and never more apparent than with property investing. As highlighted in the previous chapter you will certainly need to expect ups and downs along the way. The key is to be persistent in pursuit of your goals.

Now the thing to remember is that if you are persistent in the wrong area or strategy then this will not work either. For example if you are looking for single let properties with a high return, then investing in an area where property prices are £250,000 plus where you will get a rental yield of 5% will just not suffice. You can be as persistent as you like here, but it will just not work for you. Finding the right area for you all comes back to your individual strategy which is so important that I have dedicated a whole chapter to it in this book. There are many different strategies available in property investing, but when you have decided on yours then it is important to be persistent.

During my time in property, I have met people who have given up when they have been so close to breaking through and reaching their desired goal. This is not nice to see, and the truth is, with a little bit of persistence they would have had a whole new reality in front of them. This was the same for me when I started and fortunately as I had supportive people around me, it allowed me to keep going and break through these barriers.

The key to remember about persistence is that it is necessary in order to be successful long term. I didn't realise the importance of this at the start, and sometimes wondered what traits other successful people I was meeting had that made them achieve all they were achieving. I found persistence to be a major part of this, and let me tell you that all successful people I have met have this in abundance. I also realised that that most people have been through times when they would like to quit, and have seriously thought about it, but something or someone has kept them going.

It was no different for me. I remember when I first started out I began to approach estate agents regularly and felt initially that I was getting nowhere. I was then advertising privately for property and it seemed that with every house I went into and every seller I spoke to, there was always a reason why the property purchase would not, or could not, proceed. A specific example of this was with one particular estate agent, who I believe did not take me completely seriously when I started. This was probably because I was mid-twenties and they probably did not think I was in a position to buy property, or knew anyone who was either. How wrong they were. This particular agent is now a very good contact of mine and we often joke about the early days when I used to walk in every other day to book viewings on properties, even though I had been in there the day before and nothing changed.

Whilst this was extremely frustrating at the time, I kept going and was persistent, and I now like to think of this time as my apprenticeship. It was the time when I was putting in the groundwork and foundations for my property business, and I was creating mind space with the estate agents as well. Whilst it felt like I was initially getting nowhere with agents, I actually was because I was building relationships with them, and proving to them I was serious. This, over time, proved to be very beneficial to me and by reading this section, I would urge you to be persistent as you will get there, it can just take time and is a process.

Summary: All successful entrepreneurs and property investors are persistent. Things do not often happen overnight, so being persistent towards your goals is key. In times when you feel that you are not making moves forward, you often are, and all the work you are doing in the background will come to fruition as long as you are persistent.

18. LEVERAGE IS KEY

The concept of leveraging somebody else's time and money was an alien thought to me in 2007. I had not been party to the concept of leverage and thought as many people do, that I went to work for a period of time and got paid for the time I was there.

This all changed when I got into property and business. I learnt that you could leverage through banks, by using other people's money, and also other people's time. When I fully understood this concept, my business really made strides forward, and during this chapter we will be covering these different scenarios.

So what is leverage?

One of the definitions of leverage is, 'The ability to influence a system, or an environment, in a way that multiplies the outcome of one's efforts without a corresponding increase in the consumption of resources.' In other words, leverage is the advantageous condition of having a relatively small amount of cost, yet yielding a relatively high level of return. (Definition is taken from http://www.businessdictionary.com/definition/leverage.html)

This is an official definition of leverage. When applied to property investing, leverage can be applied in two main ways which are by using other people's time or money. I believe that leverage is so important it warranted a whole chapter, and I have personally used this successfully in my business and so wanted to share this with you.

Using other people's money

Property can be purchased with borrowed funds which is what makes it such a leveraged investment. This means that you can purchase a rental property by putting down only a percentage of the total value. Essentially, you can control the whole property and the equity it holds while only paying a fraction of its total cost. Also, the property you purchase secures the debt rather than your other assets. This is different to something such as shares where to get the benefit of £70,000 of shares you would need to invest £70,000 in cash. With property you can put in a 20% or 25% deposit and leverage the rest through a mortgage.

As mentioned earlier, you can use leverage in a variety of ways when investing in property such as buying multiple properties with one deposit, or working with other people's money.

Another question that I often get asked from people starting out with cash available is what I would do if I had money available to me, and is it best to buy one property with no mortgage or 4 or 5 properties with mortgages. Well there are definitely different options for everybody depending on your standpoint and your attitude to leverage and your risk profile. For the purpose of this example, and to keep the numbers simple, let's use £100,000 as I know in my area this could comfortably buy 4 properties currently in today's market.

One of the options is to be what is known as a cash investor. Usually what a cash investor will do is re-mortgage their own home of residence, or they may use redundancy money they have received. It is not always the case but they may have made money from property before through capital growth, and believe that the best, most risk averse, way to buy property is with no extra borrowing. They then feel that by sitting on this asset over time they will make capital growth on the property, and they are probably right, as we know historically property prices double every 7 to 10 years. This is the way they may have been told by others, and it may be the only way they feel is possible without having lots of debt and risk.

The next option for somebody with £100,000 is to split this amount up into single deposits and then take mortgage finance on the properties. This is the next stage of investing and people that use this strategy often have a different mind-set and outlook on property investing. They fully understand leverage, and also realise that there are ways to minimise risk. A seasoned property investor is always looking for ways to minimise risk, as this is extremely important for long-term profitability. I am risk averse myself and show new clients how to take the same approach as me.

So they could then split up the £100,000 into £20-25K chunks meaning they could likely buy 4 or 5 properties for their same amount of money. They can then take a mortgage for the remaining amount of the property purchase and the rent received will then service the debt on the property.

> **Important note:** This would be dependent on individual circumstances and mortgage finance available which is always different for every person. I always suggest speaking to a qualified financial advisor first to see what your mortgage availability is.

The benefit of this strategy is that you will then actually have 4 or 5 properties going up in value over time and 4 or 5 cash-flowing properties instead of one. This is vitally important to remember if you are starting out in that you can achieve cash flow through property as well as growth if you learn to buy well. This is always something I am aiming for. So, as we can see here, the mortgaged investor's return is potentially much higher as they have more assets and income for the same pot of money. If all you did was use this strategy and remain here with these four or five properties, then you would realistically have a solid part time or full time income from property, depending on your individual income goals and your investment area.

When I started out I decided to use the mortgage route and separate the money I had into separate chunks for deposits. This allowed me to buy more assets which was my strategy and plan as I wanted to build a larger portfolio. The key words I find here are *strategy* and *plan* because, as mentioned earlier, everybody will have different goals and objectives. It is important that you choose the one that is right for you.

Re-mortgaging through refinancing

Another advantage of using mortgage finance is that you can take leverage a step further when you learn to source the right kind of properties that can accommodate this. When you get to this stage your knowledge and skills will certainly become a major asset to you, and the sky is the limit.

This is because you will get to the stage that you will be able to re-finance the property or take a further advance to release your original deposit. Therefore you will able to use one deposit to buy multiple properties long term. This can happen by buying the property at a discount and adding value to the property or by the market increasing. You can then get the discounted money or the deposit back out of the property.

At the time of writing this book there have been proposed tax changes on the mortgage interest relief that will be allowed in the future, and so I suggest you contact a qualified accountant who will be able to advise you on the implications of this in relation to potential mortgage loans.

What is the difference between a re-mortgage and a further advance?

When you re-mortgage a property you transfer your

mortgage from your existing lender to another. A further advance is where you aim to borrow more money from the same lender based on the property value increasing over a period of time. The lender will need to go out and do another survey for this to happen.

Now this will only work by buying the right properties. The speed at which you can do this is also dependant on conditions at the time. Currently at the time of writing most high street lenders will expect you to have owned the property for 6 months before they will lend on it. Mortgage conditions can change and I would suggest you speak to a qualified mortgage advisor who can give you the options available to you at that time.

Leveraging using Joint venture finance

This is the ultimate form of leverage as you are potentially not using any of your own money here, but may be using your knowledge, skills and time (known as sweat equity). By using joint venture finance you potentially can buy infinite numbers of property and it is something I have experience of myself.

An example of this for me was a few years ago now. I wanted to expand but had insufficient funds to do so. I had bought a number of properties in a short timescale and so all my funds were tied up. Now it is fair to say that this does happen to many investors at some point no matter how much money you start out with. This is where I really saw the potential of using Joint venture finance. As we highlighted in a previous chapter joint ventures can happen in many different ways and I had used a variety of different types of joint venture. It really showed me the power of not having to stand still even though you may not have sufficient funds at that particular time. This form of leverage is very powerful as it means that you can potentially have multiple projects in motion at the same time if you want. Over the last few years as the economy has been so low, many people have believed that there is no money available, and everybody is struggling financially. This becomes their reality but just isn't true. There are still people making a lot of money in their business or career, and therefore they are looking to invest their excess funds in a proven long term asset such as property. This is where you can build relationships with these people, and ultimately leverage exponentially where both parties can profit.

You can also leverage other people's time which is a good tool to use especially when managing your own time.

Leveraging other people's time

For years and years I wondered why certain people seemed to get more done and make more profits in their businesses. One thing is for sure: we all have the same amount of time available to us in a day or week. The richest men and women in the world all have 24 hours in a day, the difference is that they understand leverage and have used this to their advantage.

Summary: Leverage is a key point to remember, and all successful people understand this concept fully.

19. IGNORE THE NOISE AND ONLY TAKE ADVICE FROM THOSE WHO ARE PROVEN IN PROPERTY

Over my years in property I have found that there will always be sceptics and always be reasons out there to not invest or do something. I like to call this "the noise" and I also make a conscious decision to ignore the noise.

This is one of the biggest things I have had to do over my property journey and it is quite honestly very simple to do, but is also something easy to fall back into as well. The sentence above 'only take advice from those who are proven in rental property' (and whether you choose to listen or ignore it), can quite frankly lose you or make you thousands and thousands of pounds.

I have found over my time that everyone tends to have an opinion on the property market and when it is a good time to invest. Now whilst everyone is entitled to their opinion, I would certainly urge you to think very carefully about who you take advice from. I believe that because the majority of the population buy their own home at some point, there are some people that feel that they are property experts because of this. I have found that making money from rental property is completely different, and one of the key factors in my success I feel was making sure I was only listening to people who were making money from investment property. There are a few similarities with buying your own home such as getting a good price, however there are also many differences such as rental demand, refurbishing to the required standard and not going overboard, and taking emotion out of the purchase (that is another chapter in the book).

Whilst I am very fortunate to have very supportive family and friends around me, I have definitely found from other sources that the declining property market, and 'this not being a good time to invest' has been a very popular subject for discussion. You may have been there yourself on a night out with friends at the pub, or a work night out when this has happened, and frankly they don't know what they don't know. If I had listened to this advice in 2008 then I would not have built a £multi-million portfolio, helped many other investors do the same, and I certainly wouldn't be sitting here writing this book.

I quickly learned that a little bit of knowledge for some people can be dangerous to their financial health. Now don't get me wrong I like a discussion and debate and am always open to people's ideas and suggestions. It's one of the great things in life to learn from others but I always want the person I am listening to, to have a proven track record in that field. If you wanted to learn how to play the guitar you wouldn't want to learn from someone who didn't know any chords, right?

Property is no different and as I found out to my benefit, there are many different ways to profit providing you learn from those who have been successful before you - success does leave tracks.

It also allows you to learn about the practicalities of investing and not just the theory. This has also been a real eye opener for me on my journey, as I found that learning theories and strategies is fantastic, but there is no substitute for taking action and being on the ground. By doing this it also shows you the ins and outs of investing. It will also show you that by hard work and getting the right guidance, you can achieve great results and overcome hurdles and obstacles along the way. The people who haven't experienced this will only know what they hear from outside sources, a lot of which may have come from people who have never been involved in investing themselves. Their reality may not be based on facts, but opinions from something they have heard or read about. This is definitely not the path you want to be taking. Listen to those who have achieved what you want to achieve and there is no reason you can't do the same.

I am speaking from experience here and as mentioned if I had listened to the 'doubters' in 2008 then I would not be in the position I am in today. I remember many people saying what a risky journey I was taking and that there was no money to be made out of property investment. When I scratched the surface a bit more, and asked them why they thought that, I often got two answers which were:

1. Prices are going down so you will lose a lot of money
2. What if the rent does not cover the mortgage?

Now with respect to those people, you can probably see what I mean now by their views not being based on factual information. This was how they perceived things and this was their reality as they were probably listening to all the negative media attention. If they were to go a bit deeper, then they would realise that as a professional investor we wouldn't invest if the rent did not cover the mortgage and give a healthy cash flow on top, and that buying when prices were low was actually a good thing as the key is always to buy low and sell high. They also may not realise what the current mortgage rates are for fixed mortgages and how this can allow you to know what you are paying for a mortgage for years to come. They may not understand the concepts of not being too emotional about purchases and not going overboard on a refurbishment. These are all things you get from not just the theory (which for many is not true) but the practicalities of walking the walk. This is just one example of this happening but shows that you want to be listening to people who are where you want to be. They will have walked the walk, and you want to be looking at what they do on a day-to-day basis.

I remember hearing an old saying which is 'Success leaves tracks' and it is very true. When we think about it logically, why reinvent the wheel? Now sure we all have our own personalities and traits, and our own skills we can use to our advantage. But you can also model other successful people which fast-tracks your achievements.

The concept of modelling others

The concept of modelling others is simply a process which allows you to learn from someone else's experience.

Modelling the success of others has been one of the greatest skills I have learned which has allowed me to experience so much growth in my life and business. It has made such a difference to where I was and to where I am today.

When you are trying to succeed at something, there is a better proven way to approach it. Find someone who has got the results that you desire, and model them. In school they called it "cheating", but in real-world applications it is called "smart". If you want to build a successful business, find someone else who has built a successful business and use them as a role model.

Modelling was created as a tool by people studying neurosciences who recognized that "success leaves clues". They realized that we all operate with the same fundamental skill sets, and that when you understand the organizing principles you can achieve the same results as someone else. In layman's terms, modelling is a specific process by which you can learn to achieve a desired result with less effort and less "cost" by truly learning from another person's experience.

How much faster do you think you would be able to achieve your outcome if you were able to follow a step-by-step map that had been given to you by someone who had actually achieved that specific result before? How much frustration would it save you if you could avoid the mistakes they made along the way? How much money would you save if you didn't have to fail repeatedly trying to figure out how to make it work?

This is exactly what modelling is about. It really is that simple. Success is a process that can be duplicated, and you can do this too.

> 'Experience is one of those few things you can't buy, borrow or pretend to have. It shows through!'

Summary: Unfortunately there are people out there who will want to put a dampener on your property career. This is often for many reasons including the fact they do not have the courage to act themselves. Ignore the noise, and surround yourself with people who are positive about property investing and helping you on your journey. You can also make a list of people who will be negative and what you will say to them in response. Practice these responses so they become natural and something you do to keep positive and block out any unwanted interference. Model people with experience and who have got the results you want, and you can duplicate their success.

20. EMBRACE A CHANGING MARKET AND ALWAYS KEEP LEARNING

There is one thing you can definitely know for certain with property investment and that is that the market is constantly changing. Whether that be a change in interest rates or other market conditions there will always be changes to embrace. However with change comes opportunity and it is your job as a Property Investor to profit regardless of what is happening. And you really can, no matter what others say.

When I began in 2008, the interest rates suddenly dropped as we had one of the worst recessions in history. After researching the market and learning from those who were already doing it, I began to quickly realise that this would be a great time to purchase high cash-flowing assets, at rock bottom prices.

Now it was a shock when this happened and I did have the crisis thoughts and feelings about whether it really was a good time to invest. All the news and media were painting a very negative picture about the economy and the property market in general. I was feeling a bit torn initially, but then decided wholeheartedly to ignore the noise and take advice from others who were investing and making a profit.

It was a big decision but I genuinely thought at the time that if I didn't do it then, I never would. I am sure you can resonate with this when you have done something in your life that is a big decision, but you thought if I don't do it now then I will regret it for a long time. This is how I felt. When I looked at other people around me who were being successful, and focused on the other stories of people getting life-changing results in property, I also thought to myself, "What is the worst that can happen?" This is going to be a very big change for me but if for any reason it didn't work I could always go and get another job. Now I didn't think about this for too long as I wanted to remain positive, but I always err on the side of caution and I wanted a plan B just in case.

So how do we combat a changing market?

I learnt early on that diversity was the key to any successful business or investment. I also realised that when markets changed I would need to adapt with these changes to continue to be profitable. I always thought though that with change comes opportunity and there are always ways to profit providing you know how.

One of the ways I combat a changing market is by keeping my knowledge up to date. As markets change, it is vitally important to keep up to date with the latest strategies and changes that are occurring regularly. For example at the time of writing this book there are proposed tax changes in 2017 which will mean that you cannot claim all of your mortgage interest as has previously been the case. There has also been a new stamp duty law brought in for April 2016 which means that individuals will need to pay an extra 3% on all property purchases, dependant on circumstances.

Now I would obviously suggest that you speak to a qualified accountant about this, but keeping up to date with these changes means you can be proactive rather than reactive which is key. As always, there will be people who will now focus on these changes and say that it will stop property being a profitable investment. The reality is that it still will be profitable and certainly if you are in it for the long term. It may mean there is a fluctuation in prices or that we have to negotiate a bit harder, but long term it will still be profitable as long as you factor in these extra costs, and stick to the core fundamentals and rules.

Similarly the mortgage market is always changing, and so keeping in regular contact with a mortgage broker is also key to understanding what changes there are in the market.

Change also becomes easier to handle when you always keep learning more. If you continue to learn and develop then you will be able to embrace change and see the opportunities that arise because of it. You never know it all and can always learn more as you go along.

One of the biggest traits I have found in successful property or business people is their ability to always keep learning. The minute we think we know it all is the moment we are on the decline.

> 'There is a saying, 'if you are green you grow and if you are ripe you rot', and we don't want to be the ones who rot.

I make this a constant factor in my business and am always trying to learn on a daily basis. It is not only important for me, but also means that I can pass this onto the people I coach and mentor now.

So what tools do I use to keep learning?

There are many ways you can keep learning and below are some of the main ways that I do this.

1. Online portals and material

In this day and age, as mentioned earlier there is so much information out there online, meaning that you can learn constantly through newsletters, blogs, videos, reports and other things that are online and accessible.

2. Offline networking

Although there is so much information online, it is still important to network regularly offline as well, as they both complement each other. There is often no substitute for face to face interaction and this can be found at property networking events and all business networking events where you can learn lots of information on systems and processes and running the day to day business as well which is very important. Many property networking events not only have the opportunity to network, but they also have a guest speaker each month on different topics. Therefore you can build your knowledge this way and research which events sound appealing to you.

3. Peers and other support groups

Over the years I have learnt so much from my peers and other groups I have been part of. Whether that is an online forum or a group of people who meet regularly for a drink and a chat, it all helps as you learn from other people's experiences. Therefore you don't just learn the theory but the reality as well, which is crucial to your success.

4. Trade conferences and investment shows

There are various conferences and investment shows throughout the year. These will often be big events where hundreds of people come together over at least a few days. You will be able to listen to people share their stories, attend seminars that are being run, and network with many others who are active in property. These are the kind of places that you can learn from people who are walking the walk and using the latest strategies, therefore building on the knowledge you currently have.

Summary: By embracing a changing market it means that you can see the opportunities that many others can't when they fear this change. Always keep learning though to make sure you stay ahead of the game.

21. AIM FOR MORE THAN ONE TENANT TYPE WHEN INVESTING

When looking at property in the early days I used to look at the price, do my due diligence, and look at rental demand which are all good things to be doing and very important. However as I went along, and to further minimise risk, I wanted to make sure that there was more than one tenant type available to rent the property I was buying.

So what does this mean?

Now one of my rules is that I like the property to work as a both a single let or a multi-let property if possible. This therefore means that if you were planning for the property to be a multi-let rented to students for example, that it would also work financially should it have to be a single let for any reason. Now on this basis you would have two tenant types available, potentially a family and students. However I like to adhere to this with all properties where I can. If I use my portfolio as an example, then I have properties that I could rent to an LHA family (a family on benefits), a private family who are working, or even potentially a company let or HMO. If it is an HMO property I could rent to either students, working professionals, or again potentially a company let. Therefore on all my properties I am aiming for as many different potential tenant types as possible, which makes me feel better about things, but also minimises the risk of voids, which is very important!.

As mentioned where possible I always like the property to work as both a single let and a multi-let as well.

For example if I was to buy a four-bed property at £110,000 and rent the rooms individually, I would likely make in the region of £350-£400 per month per room in my area, based on current rents. Now this would be my main strategy, however if for any reason I could not rent the rooms individually, then the property would still wash its face as a single let, or make a smaller cash flow. Now whilst this is not ideal, it would not be a complete disaster. If I was to buy a bigger property at £200,000 then it would likely not work as a single let, and you would have to rent the rooms individually to be profitable. This is just something to think about and the more tenant types you have available the better it is to minimise risk.

Summary: Aiming for more than one tenant really minimises your risk when investing in property. Whilst you may have a preferred tenant type which you should aim for, making sure there are other options if needed will ensure you are safeguarding your investment over time.

22. INVEST FOR CASH FLOW AND RETURN – CAPITAL GROWTH IS THE ICING ON THE CAKE

I certainly cannot stress this particular point enough and it is a point that all successful property and business people follow diligently. Back before the crash in 2008, we were in a rising market where property prices were going up every year and investors were being able to buy properties and re-mortgage them straight away, in some cases the same day. This was seen as a fantastic time to invest and property was hot in the media and on TV, with many programmes on how to profit in the rental market, and how to buy and sell for profit. Those who were seasoned, had knowledge, and were willing to take action, were building large successful portfolios.

Unfortunately though, there was the other side of the coin and some of the people that were just relying on capital growth found themselves in trouble. Because it was seemingly easy to attract finance and buy lots of properties, some investors were taking their eye off the ball with regards to cash flow and return. This was distressing for some as they bought properties often because they could, but did not follow the golden rules of stress testing every investment rigorously. When the crash happened, they found that they had overstretched and many of the properties just didn't achieve the rental returns they needed to cash flow their business. In more extreme cases certain investors had huge void periods, and with no equity in the property they found that the profitability of their investment had gone.

This really taught me that cash-flow was king, and capital growth was not to be completely relied upon. Going back to the Dragon's Den analogy I referred to earlier in the book, you can see that cash-flow is extremely important to high value business people as well. They are investing in the person which is another important point, but from a business point of view they want to see that the business works from a cash-flow perspective and want to know when if they invest let's say £50,000, they will get it back.

Property investing should be no different and as mentioned in a previous chapter it should be treated like a business. Therefore you should always be looking at monthly cash flow, and return on investment.

So what does this mean?

Well, as mentioned earlier cash flow from a property is calculated by taking the monthly rent and subtracting the monthly costs. These costs can include mortgage payments, insurances, service charges if applicable, management fees, and incidental funds.

Return on investment is calculated by taking the annual cash-flow and dividing it by the total costs put into the property.

So for the purpose of this example let's say that you had to put £25,000 into a property purchase. This covered your deposit, refurbishment, and buying costs associated with purchasing the property. You then buy a property which makes you £400 per month cash-flow so £4,800 for the year. You would then make a 19.2 % return on your investment which is calculated by dividing £4,800 by £25,000. Not bad I am sure you will agree when you may only get 2 to 3% in a bank.

This is certainly an achievable target in my area, and in some cases the returns are higher depending on the property strategy.

These however are the figures that a seasoned investor would want to know. They are treating each property purchase as a business entity, which is key. Now it is your job as an investor to track these properties and keep regular records of the return the property is making you in reality. There is the theory and then there is the reality and let's say you have a couple of void months or some increased costs, then the actual return will decrease. This is why it is important to put an incidental fund in there, and not be too generous on your figures. If you allow for unexpected things to happen and the return is still good, then if they don't then it is an added bonus. You should still make a healthy return and by setting up your investments in this way you are preparing like a seasoned investor. Don't get me wrong: when you achieve capital growth then this is a fantastic bonus, but the investment has to work on a monthly basis for you to be able to see the capital growth in the years to come.

Summary: Successful entrepreneurs and property investors invest for cash-flow and see this as a big priority. Whilst you make money when you buy and we want capital growth, cash flow is what will see you through any hard times you may face.

23. NO EMOTION

Keeping my emotions out of my property purchases was a key lesson I learnt from a previous mentor of mine, and when I did I found it to be very beneficial to my investments. This was because I learnt to be objective about them and not subjective.

I covered earlier in the book the importance of rules when making investment decisions. One of the biggest problems I have seen with people new to property is that they fail to detach their emotions from their investment. This can seriously affect profits as it means that people will do things with their investments that they just do not need to do. I often see people start out by asking themselves, "Would I live here?" and it is certainly not a question you should be asking yourself. One of the key points to remember in any property investment purchase is that you are not living there, and your choice of curtains or carpets is not likely to make a difference at all.

Another way emotions can play a part is when someone is struggling to find good leads or properties. Sometimes people can buy things they would normally turn down. It's a trap I warn my mentees about, and one I have nearly fallen foul of myself. When you are desperate or frustrated you are more prone to making rash decisions, but I would urge you not to. Stick to your rules as highlighted before, and trust in your buying model based on your rules. Then your emotions will not come into play and you will make sound business decisions, which is what I do.

It wasn't always that way for me though. When I was new to property I found myself initially falling into this trap and being too emotional about the whole buying process and worrying when there were not as many leads coming through. I began to think about whether I would live in certain properties, and also there was the element of wanting to tell friends I was buying in nicer areas of town, rather than the ones that were actually profitable and gave me the highest return.

This mind shift for many can be hard but when done can boost profits entirely.

So what should we be thinking?

You should always be looking at your property investments as an investment vehicle and not as a trophy to show people. You should always be looking at which property will give you the highest return for your chosen strategy. Now this does not mean looking for the lowest price property because as discussed sometimes the figures look great, but it could be in the worst area of town which gives you no end of trouble. It is about getting a balance and what I call the 'sweet spot' which is not looking for the worst property, but certainly not looking for the most physically attractive property either. That way you can keep your mind on the numbers and whether the figures stack up as a solid investment. What your friends or anyone else thinks of how it looks on the surface does not count at all. Each property you buy moves you closer to your financial goal and the lifestyle you want and deserve. Property can be strange in the fact that one month you will have a lot less leads than another month, but it is important to stay positive and wait for suitable properties to come through, as if you buy hastily then you could make a bad purchase which could affect you for years to come.

Summary: Being emotional about property purchases is a big mistake. Look at property in an objective way, not a subjective way. This will be far more profitable than letting your emotions get the better of you.

24. MASTER ONE STRATEGY BEFORE MOVING ON

Now I want to be brutally honest here, as I feel that this is something that is very important to your success. It is also something that allows you to avoid overwhelm and confusion. I cannot stress the importance of mastering one strategy first, and making sure that your systems and processes are all in working order.

Before I started investing in 2007 I did what many other people do when they are looking into a new project or career. I began to read up on property as much as I could, be it through books, eBooks, or other journals, both online and offline. Whilst this was fantastic and really opened my eyes, it was also a real insight into the amount of different strategies that were out there for me to choose from. I was like a kid in a candy shop and I was thinking about which one to choose and which one I was going to pursue first. It was at this point I remember speaking to my mentor who gave me what turned out to be priceless advice. "Pete, master one strategy before moving on," was what she said. I remember sitting there at the time not really knowing the value of what she had said to me. It was something that I initially really struggled with and had to really train myself to do. I have always been an ambitious person, which is good because it allows me to think big and I always try to improve on the current knowledge and skills that I already have. The downside of this is that my mind did wander at the start and

I was looking at many different strategies and ideas that I had with property investment. What I found though is that if I tried to do too much and grab too much, I didn't really achieve what I wanted, and just found myself with a sense of overwhelm and confusion. I really learnt from this experience and found that the best way was to focus on one thing first and get it systemised before moving on.

> Important note: Research, educate yourself and master one strategy before looking for the next challenge. Don't get distracted by the latest fad as it may not be right for you at that current time. Only when one strategy is mastered should you think about the next steps.

A good thing to consider is the 80/20 rule (Pareto's law) which states that 80% of results (both universally and personally) are achieved from 20% of the total time input. 80% of the money is made by 20% of people, and 80% of your money is made in 20% of your time. This is an amazing rule and one that you should apply when looking at where you spend your time.

I always suggest that people starting out make a point of learning as much as possible about the strategy that excites them the most and focus on this. Now there have been various strategies covered in this book and there are often new ones coming to the market, but to find the one that you want to focus on first you can ask yourself questions such as:

1. What did I get into property investment for?

2. Realistically how much time do I currently have to dedicate to my property business?
3. What parts of property am I most interested in?
4. Do I enjoy the hands on side of property or the business management side?
5. What strategies can I realistically use based on my current financial position?

These are just a handful of the questions you can ask yourself to get a clear picture of which strategy you want to focus on first. This should stop your mind from wandering and looking at what others are doing, which may just drain your time and hinder your progress.

Summary: Mastering one strategy before moving on is a vital part of your development. Trying to do too many strategies in one go can cause overwhelm and confusion. In addition to this, when you try to do too many strategies at once, you often will not be giving each one the attention it requires to get to the position you want. Make sure you master one and get it systemised correctly before moving on.

25. DELAYED GRATIFICATION

Delayed gratification is a concept that is not always followed by a lot of people. You know the drill, your friend gets a pay rise at work, or maybe inherits some money, (there are many other scenarios as well) and decides to go straight out and buy a new car, or new wardrobe and expensive holiday. This in my opinion is not the best way and delayed gratification is something that should be adhered to for a period of time.

So what is this?

The definition of delayed gratification, or deferred gratification, is the ability to resist the temptation for an immediate reward and wait for a later, much better, reward. Generally, delayed gratification is associated with resisting a smaller but more immediate reward in order to receive a larger or more enduring reward later.

Another way to describe this is to "Have Your Cake and Save it For Later", and essentially do not get greedy!

It is a shame but time and time again people burn their chances of long-term wealth because of their need for instant gratification.

Sometimes it is not their fault as seminars or success stories can entice you in with the glitzy promise of instant riches and wealth. What you need to remember is a lot of the time these people have used delayed gratification themselves and followed this process. It is often just easier for them to sell their services based on making it sound easy to achieve instant money and success. This can happen in lots of different business arenas, and wealth creation models, not just property.

The key to long term wealth is to utilise the law of compounding.

The key I have found is to definitely let your assets grow by compounding your earnings so that your asset base becomes large enough to pay you for the rest of your life.

I remember having to use this rule and theory an awful lot in my first couple of years in property, and it actually came into effect on the week I was leaving my job to go full time in property. It is an incident I will never forget and actually quite funny now although it wasn't at the time. I was investing heavily in the property business at the time and any spare money I had was going into the business. I was driving a Rover 200 at the time which let's just say had a tenancy to be temperamental and not start very well on a cold day. I remember going out to the car park when I finished work for what I thought would be a straightforward drive home, but how wrong I was. Where I worked was a big place with hundreds of employees and it was not a small car park by any means. So as I got closer to my car I was already a tiny bit embarrassed as the driver side lock was already broken so I had to let myself in through the passenger seat. So as I proceeded to do this I then realised that the car would not start after four or five attempts to do so. I have to admit at the time I was embarrassed and the noise the car was making was certainly getting me some attention. After numerous further attempts to start the car it was not getting any better and what followed was me having to ring to be hotwired out of the car park. You can imagine the shame!

Just days earlier, people I had known at work for a long time had been asking me what I was leaving for and what other job I had got. I subsequently said that I was leaving to start my own property investment business, and I can still see the looks on their faces, especially as the car I was driving was probably worth less than the holidays they had just been on.

On a serious note however, it did teach me about delayed gratification and the importance of this. Now I certainly was not flush at the time by any means, but I was in a position to go out and buy a better car than this old Rover. However, I didn't do that; instead I made sacrifices to follow my goals and dreams and I am very glad that I did. I bought my favourite car 2 years later.

> Important note: The truth is that you can have the nice things, but it may just take longer. When you do however it is not a stretch and you can then afford them comfortably.

So I would always say to do the following when starting out, so that you can secure your long-term financial future and wealth:

- Avoid taking all of your money out of a deal too early or gearing up too high [borrowing extra cash at the cost of high repayment rates], as it will damage your long term wealth.

- It is very rare that we get something for nothing, and this is certainly the case with borrowed money.

- Borrowed money should be treated with absolute respect, and your long term credit file treated the same way, so that you can maximise leverage for the long term. I am always looking at mid to long term investment strategies: compounding growth and cash to ensure long-term sustainability and security.

- This is a mind-set as much as it is a strategy, and thinking in this way will dramatically increase your chances of being where you want to be for the rest of your life.

- Avoid spending all of your profits straight away on the finer things in life. Be patient, delay gratification and you will have long term wealth, freedom and security. The goal in all of this is to hold out until your asset base can pay you for generations to come.

Hopefully you can see the power of that.

Summary: Delayed gratification is key to your success. Be patient, delay gratification and you will have long-term wealth, freedom and security.

26. BELIEVE AND HAVE FAITH IN YOURSELF

I was always taught from an early age that you need to believe and have faith in yourself. You need to find a compelling reason to do what you do but then believe completely in what you are trying to achieve.

It is often said that anything you ever achieve in your life is because you have had some kind of faith in yourself, and you trusted yourself that you could and would achieve it, therefore you had faith in your instinct and intuition. Now no one said it would be easy, and there are times when it will be hard to have continued faith in yourself, especially if you have not currently seen the results you want. You can however achieve your goals if you have continued faith and belief, and keep moving forward.

> Important note: You have to raise your ceiling of belief in what you think you can do or achieve. If you do this every day then you will condition yourself into aiming higher, and therefore you will have more belief in yourself that you can achieve more, and will then likely do so.

The truth is that you may be the only one (certainly at the start) who believes you can buy profitable properties and that they even exist in today's market. You may be the only person who believes that there are multiple strategies and ways to profit in property, and no one else is going to do this for you. Keep going and following your dream, no matter what outside influences may say.

I have also seen many people get cold feet before their first property purchase. They have done all the hard work and then, just at the time they are about to commit to the purchase, they lose faith. Don't let this happen to you as it often can be your mind playing tricks on you so that you doubt yourself. Remember you have done the due diligence and hard work to find the property, and if it works based on your criteria and rules, there is no reason to not move forward with it.

Summary: Believe in yourself and your abilities to succeed. Have faith in yourself and trust yourself and your instincts to make the right decisions most of the time, and you will.

27. PAYING YOUR ENTRANCE FEE

I feel that this is an important point to stress for people who are starting out their journey in property. This is because I feel that sometimes property can be portrayed to be a quick and easy get rich scheme. This is where I feel a lot of people fall down as they are often expecting results to be instant. This can be a big mistake and sometimes instant results are not solid, and can go as quickly as they have come. Now this is not to say that you cannot make progress quickly, but sometimes the end result you are looking for takes times and patience. That is where the saying 'paying your entrance fee' comes in to play. What I mean here is that property investing is like any other thing that you want to get good at or master in that it takes time, effort, and your full commitment. I personally see that this needs to happen in two ways, and was certainly what all successful investors I have met have done previously.

1. Paying your entrance fee with your time and commitment

This is vitally important and will come in the form of many different things, such as networking with other people interested in property, spending time with estate agents, and constantly viewing properties as well. Many people can fall down just because of this point as life can get in the way and people find they are too busy. Now many people are busy in life but to be successful in property we need to make this one of the important priorities to spend as much time as we can on it, especially in the early days. I found this to be case when I started as well. I was working full-time, was running my own home, and had many other things that had to be done that kept me busy. I did, however, use every bit of free time I had (evenings and weekends) on property which meant I could develop and maintain relationships with agents and other investors, which proved very fruitful and still is to this day. You will find that as you become more experienced and have more contacts you may need to view less properties and spend less time visiting agents as they already know you and you have built the trust and relationship. You may then be full time in property giving you more time that you can dedicate, but at the start you will still have to spend time ' paying your entrance fee' which can be time consuming, especially if you work full-time as well. If you stick with it, and put this time in, then you should find it very valuable in the long-term.

2. Financially paying your entrance fee

The second way that you will often need to pay your entrance fee is in a financial way. Now this does not mean that you have to spend thousands on courses that sell the dream, and do not deliver, and then find yourself with no money left, feeling let down and miss-sold to. What I mean by this is that you will have to pay to attend networking events, travelling to meet people, travelling to view properties, amongst other things. You may then decide to attend trainings and courses investing in yourself which I do feel is very important at the right time for you. If you decide to do this then it is very important to pick the training or mentor that is right for you (as covered in an earlier chapter), and make sure you do your due diligence on who you decide to work with. There are sometimes people out there who cannot understand why someone would pay for property education. Well my answer to that is always that people pay for a variety of courses on other topics, and people spend thousands going to university each year, as I did myself. Now while this is good if this is what you want to do, it is still a good idea to get trained and invest in your education if property investment is what you want to do. I would always urge people to not listen to those people, as getting educated will put you a step ahead of the game, and fast track progress. There are some very good trainings and mentors out there, so it is just a case of picking the one you feel is right for you. Whichever way you decide to proceed, it is important to realise that there will be a cost implication when getting into property investment, but this should be looked at as investing for future gains.

Summary: Property is like any new career or journey that you decide to take. You will need to pay your entrance fee and serve an 'apprenticeship', metaphorically speaking. This means that you will need to put time and effort in, and also some financial input, but long term your opportunities and rewards can be mind-blowing.

28. NEGOTIATION

Negotiation is a key skill that every aspiring business person or property investor needs to learn to be successful. If I'm honest it was something I did not particularly enjoy when I first started in property, but soon realised that it was something I would need to embrace and get good at to survive in the business. As mentioned in a previous chapter, being ethical in the negotiation process was of paramount importance to me. I have however learned some key points about the negotiation process that this chapter will highlight, whether that be negotiating with a private seller, an estate agent, or anyone else in your business for that matter.

There are many difference stages of negotiation which we will be covering more in this chapter. These include:

- Explaining to the other party why you are there
- Allowing them to fully explain their circumstances
- Listening intently
- Clearly reaffirming back to them what they have said, so you both understand each other
- Explaining and framing what your offer may be
- Giving alternatives to them
- Listening again to them and then further negotiation if needed

As you can see listening is there twice as this is a very important stage. They always say that you have two ears and one mouth for a reason. There are different things needed to negotiate well and ethically with the vendor or the agent, and we will be covering these in further detail now.

Negotiation with sellers

There are many different ways to source profitable property investments which we covered earlier. These different ways will fall into two categories which are: dealing with estate agents and dealing with private vendors. Whilst the negotiation aspect of these will carry some similarities, they will also have distinct differences and this section will highlight some of the main differences to look for, and will allow you to deal with each scenario in the correct way.

The basic principles of negotiation

Negotiation is certainly an art that can be taught and every successful investor will have learnt and mastered this art to the best of their ability.

Buying a property is one of the most expensive transactions you are likely to make, so it is important to do it right and get the best price possible.

There are many factors that will determine the price of a property, varying from demand in the area to any defects it has. So, especially with prices steadily increasing, it is worth taking stock to ensure you are getting value for money, and to ensure you are negotiating to the best of your ability.

The importance of listening skills in negotiation

This can be the hardest part of the process for many people, but is often the most important and when you can learn the most. Some of the best deals I have done have come from just listening to someone's circumstances, and letting them tell me what they want. Sometimes I have not even had to make an offer to strike a mutually beneficial deal.

Often when people feel they can help someone or have the answer, there can be a tendency to try and put everything in your offer across in one go. This can sometimes be due to nerves as well if you are new to the situation, but you have to have faith that you will get your time to put everything across that you want to. If you do want to say something that seems relevant when the other person is talking but are afraid you may forget, then write it down, but do not interrupt them as this is a big mistake.

Interrupting someone can lose rapport in an instant. Every stage of negotiation is important, but this one can be most crucial. If you get this right and become a good listener, you will be amazed how it can transform your negotiating skills and results.

Drivers that can make the vendor motivated

Before negotiating it is important to understand the 'drivers' that can make vendors motivated. If a seller is not motivated, then you can be the best negotiator in the world with Jedi mind tricks and it still will not work. It is important to remember that motivation comes in many different ways, not just financial.

Some of the main ways are:

- Probate
- Relocation
- Redundancy or loss of Job
- Divorce
- Cash flow problems

The importance of certainty when negotiating

As human beings we all want to feel certain about our situations. We want to be certain that we can pay our mortgage and bills, and put food on the table for our children. Similarly a vendor wants to be certain that their house sale will complete once it has been agreed. They may be in a very stressful position and by buying their property you are solving their problem.

Property can be fraught with uncertainty though and it can never be one hundred per cent certain. Things can happen during the selling process that cannot be accounted for, and sometimes this does happen, and a potential seller could have been subject to a sale falling through before. It is our job as investors though to make the process as certain as possible for a vendor when buying their property, and not mess them around or keep them waiting. This is a very important part of the negotiation and not to be underestimated. Your offer is likely to carry a lot more weight if the vendor is certain. There are different ways to do this including it being a fast cash sale, or by having a mortgage already secured and instructing solicitors quickly. This gives them more certainty and they are less likely to want to look elsewhere. This business is about solving people's problems. When we understand the person's needs in front of us, we can then offer the right solution.

Negotiating with an estate agent

To begin with, it is important to remember that an agent must pass on any offer you make to the vendor of a property.

Some areas are so popular with potential buyers that you will get pushed into a sealed bid, where buyers make one confidential bid on a property.

However, while there is nothing wrong with going in low, going in too low may annoy the seller, especially when you are up against other buyers.

I truly believe the key when it comes to negotiating with the agent, is not to shoot yourself in the foot and go in with too high an offer at the start.

Most agents won't expect the buyer to offer the asking price from the outset and will be ready and prepared to negotiate.

If you go in too high you'll have no room to manoeuvre when it comes to negotiating.

When looking to negotiate with estate agents I follow a strategic plan, and below are some of the main rules that I adhere to.

1. Be appealing as a buyer

This may seem obvious, but when there is lots of competition for a property it helps if you can sell yourself as a buyer. To start with, an agent is going to be more attracted to your offer if you can move quickly. This is also very important if you are a first-time landlord as the agent will want to be confident that you can deliver on your promise. You can put yourself in a strong position to do this by making sure that you have a mortgage in principle approved.

If you haven't, it would certainly be a good idea to do so and check first as this is something that an estate agent may ask you for from the outset. When it comes to negotiating on price you want to make yourself appealing as a buyer.

For example, chains are a nightmare when it comes to a property transaction. The longer the chain, the more complicated the completion process is likely to be and the more likely the whole process will fall apart.

If you're not in a chain then use this to your advantage to negotiate on price. It means you're a much stronger buyer on paper, as there is a much smaller probability that problems will arise up to the point of completion.

2. Do not be too overpowering to begin with – aim to build rapport

Estate agents will likely be approached daily by investors looking for buy to let property and in that sense you will be no different. One common mistake that new investors make is to be too overpowering and ask estate agents for hugely discounted properties. This is a huge mistake when negotiating and will turn the agent off straight away. The key at the start is to build rapport and get to know them personally to begin with. This will build credibility and trust and give you a much better chance in the negotiation process.

3. Act in an efficient timely manner

One of the key parts of negotiation and what can set you aside from the rest is that you act in a timely, efficient manner. This can get overlooked in the negotiation process but it is a very important part of it. The key when dealing with an agent is to get your survey booked as soon as possible, and then keep them up to date with timescales and a likely completion date for the property. Failure to keep the agent up to date with progress will mean that you risk the chance of the property falling through, or of jeopardising your relationship with them.

> Important note: Be a closer not a poser. Don't keep the agent hanging on, or mess them around by not closing the deal. They will not appreciate this and it can burn a relationship very quickly that you have spent time building. Be honest and if you can't proceed let them know quickly so they can carry on marketing the property.

4. Always back up your offer with a sound financial argument

When dealing with estate agents it is key to back up any offer you make with a sound financial argument. Your first offer should certainly not be so far under the asking price that the vendor doesn't take you seriously, but close enough that they will come back with a counter offer and engage in a negotiation. It is important to not get too emotional about your purchase even if you really want the property. It's common for negotiations to go back and forth several times, so hold your nerve and keep your maximum price in mind. This is key as you will want to have a ceiling price that you are prepared to pay for a property.

Once you've finalised the price negotiations, you can then agree on the conditions of purchase, such as the settlement time and finance approval if you need to.

5. Be prepared to walk away if needed

As professional investors we regularly talk about walking away from our investments if needed. This is key as we need to work to a strict criteria when making offers and purchasing properties. The criteria each investor has can be different depending on many factors (these were covered in a chapter before), however the principle of walking away if it isn't right remains the same.

This is very important and is vital in your negotiation. This is not to say that you can't negotiate and bend slightly, however you must have a top line. This top line would be the maximum you are prepared to pay for the property based on your due diligence and criteria, and divorced from any urges to increase that 'little bit more' to agree the sale. This would effectively mean that if your calculations bring you to an investment offer of £100,000 you should not be pushed into upping your offer more. If your top line is £100,000 there is nothing wrong with starting at £95,000 and then increasing from there if you have to. What you don't want to do is keep increasing above the £100,000 in order to secure the sale. We have seen this happen many times in the past and it can be financially damaging and eat into your bottom line. The estate agent's job is to get as much as they can for the property, however you have to work out what it is worth to you and be prepared to walk away should it not be enough. The mistake some new investors make is to not walk away and it will actually harm your relationship with the agent as they will see you as someone who they can coerce into always offering more. The key is to stick to your plan and strategy, and long term this will build credibility and gain respect from the agent, as they will see you as someone who is a serious investor.

Negotiating with private vendors of properties carries a lot of the same rules as dealing with estate agents however there are some distinct differences to bear in mind. Below are some of these key differences.

1. You will likely not have an asking price to take into consideration

By the very basis of a private sale, it means that the vendor may not have put the property on the market. They will however probably have a figure in their head which they want to achieve from the sale. When there is an estate agent involved with the sale, the owner of the property will likely use their valuation as the basis for their judgement. This is not always the way as some properties are priced to sell and in some cases estate agents price the property higher.

2. The agent will likely have already found out their lowest figure

When sourcing through an estate agent, they will already have found out from the seller what their ideal price is and what they are willing to accept for the property. This may well be reflected in the asking price for the property. When sourcing through private vendors you will not have the information from the outset, and will need to find this out for yourself. It is very possible the private seller has come to you after they have not had any joy selling through an agent. Therefore you may still have the agent's asking price to contend with. If this is the case you can use this as a starting point, but you will still need to do your own homework, due diligence and only offer what fits your strategy and price range. If this is not enough for the seller then thank them and walk away. If they don't sell, over time they may come back to you (this has happened many times to me). If the property has not sold through the agent, then it is likely that the asking price is too high and that is something you can use in the negotiations with them.

3. Use multiple strategies in the negotiations and give more than one option

One key point in the negotiations with a private seller is that you can use multiple strategies and give the seller different options. This is very powerful and is not always possible when negotiating with an estate agent. This is because the agent might not understand creative strategies such as lease options. They may not understand them or not want to deal with them even if they do.

Therefore the negotiations with agents can be very straight down the line. With private vendors this may be different and you may be able to introduce different options for them:

As an example let's refer to the case study below:

You go to see a private seller who believes their house is worth is £105k, and they are only willing to accept £90k as a lowest figure. Let's say you have done your due diligence and have come to your top figure of £80k. Many investors may walk away at this point if the seller will not accept this and at the start of my investing career I did the same. It is safe to say that I had potentially left thousands and thousands of pounds on the table. So here are some different ways to give the seller more than one option.

1. You can explain to the seller that you can only offer £80k and leave this option on the table. The seller might well come back to you if they don't achieve the £90k they want.

2. You can offer £80k but make it a cash sale if possible and inform the seller this should only take 2 weeks dependent on solicitors. This essence of speed may be enough to seal the deal at £80k if they are motivated.

3. You can look at creative strategies such as an assisted sale – offer the vendor £90k and take an option on the property for a period of time. You can then try and find a buyer for the property using an estate agent, and if you can achieve £95 to £100k through them you can take this bit in the middle or split this with an agent. This is a win/win as the seller gets what they want and you are also able to profit from the situation.

4. You could offer the seller a lease option. Therefore you agree to give the seller £90k or even £95-100k but in 3, 5, or 7 years' time.

So what is a lease option?

A lease option (more formally Lease with the Option to Purchase) is a type of contract used in both residential and commercial real estate. In a lease-option, a property owner and tenant agree that, at the end of a specified rental period for a given property, the renter has the option of purchasing the property. When the term expires, the renter must either exercise or forfeit the purchase option. A lease option gives a renter/potential buyer more flexibility than a lease-purchase agreement, which requires the renter to purchase the property at the end of the rental period. Lease options is a strategy that I cover in more detail with my students and mentees.

These are all different options you can give to a private vendor, and as you can see there are many different options available. By giving this to the seller it is a way to gauge their motivation without having to negotiate too hard which some people do not like to do. You can let the vendor know that you cannot give a timescale on all the different options, but your offer of £80k will be a guaranteed sale and the process will be quick as you already have a mortgage in place. It may be the case (which has happened to us) that the vendor decides that speed is of the essence and they will accept £80k or say "Well if you can get me £82k or £83k, then we have a deal." You then have a decision to make as to whether you feel that you can stretch to that, but you have still brought the price down by showing them different ways, and trust me this is very powerful.

4. They may have had previous sales that have fallen through previously

If a private seller contacts you through your different means of advertising and says that they have had a few sales fall through, this puts you in a strong position. Now I certainly do not believe that we should ever take advantage of a seller because of this, and I believe in being totally transparent and ethical in all situations. However if a seller has had sales fall through then they may tell you the price and this then gives you a starting point which you otherwise would not have. We have found in the past that there is often room for negotiation on this figure if you can provide a fast, efficient sale. If the seller is motivated, the previous sales falling through will potentially make the seller move on price if you can act quickly.

In all cases the key is to build rapport first before talking about any financial scenarios. Many people think that the negotiation process has to be some long, drawn out ten-hour conversation with backs against the wall and this can be very off-putting for many including myself. In reality, some of the best property deals I have done have been through building rapport and trust with a vendor or agent, and by seeing how I can help. If I can establish a win/win then great, and if we cannot reach an agreement then it is important to thank them for their time and move on. You can always leave your offer on the table if circumstances change, and wish them the best of luck. This is what I like to do.

Summary: As you can see, negotiation is a very important part of your property journey. It is something that must be mastered to be successful in property and business. When you do so you will be able to ethically negotiate a win/win situation for both parties, meaning that you will be able to profit and help others too. When you do negotiate always offer more than one option which gives more chance of achieving a win/win situation. This has been a great tool to use in the negotiation process for me, and something that can show that you are trying to be flexible in giving different ways to help.

MISTAKES TO AVOID LIKE THE PLAGUE

Over my time in property I have seen what I believe to be common mistakes that certain people have made and this chapter will highlight the most common mistakes for you to avoid.

1. Giving up

Unfortunately I have seen many people give up, just at the point when all the hard work they have done is about to come to fruition, and things are about to start happening for them.

It seems many people want instant results. People expect these instant results and are often 'sold this expectation', and so it is a trap many can fall into. When this doesn't happen they get bored, disillusioned, sick and tired of it all and then move onto something else. Unfortunately they often then go through the same cycle all over again.

The reason that 99% of people fail is because they give up. You only fail when you give up.

This is such a simple concept that we all know, but as soon as things get a little bit tough, most people can't stand the heat and they leave the kitchen. They are always looking for the easiest most comfortable solution.

Many successful entrepreneurs have said in the past that if

you are comfortable with everything you are doing then you are not stretching yourself. Things need to be uncomfortable at times, you need to step outside your comfort zone, and then you know you are pushing yourself and you are growing.

2. Lack of flexibility

The market is always changing, and the economy is always changing. The environment is always changing and it is important that we move with these changes.

The market is different this year to what it was last year, and there have been radical changes since the start of the recession. We need to move with these changes to always stay one step ahead.

3. Being too emotional

This particular subject has been mentioned earlier in the book, but I feel it is that important that I need to mention it again. It is something that unfortunately prevents many people from making the profits they should. It may not be something that comes naturally to you, and you may find yourself wanting to fall back into the habit of looking at what you want from a property, or what you want the property to look like. This is financially disastrous and as mentioned can end up costing you money that you do not need to pay out.

By looking at your property purchases objectively and as an investment vehicle, it will mean that you will not make emotional decisions, and you will make more financially sound decisions.

4. Lack of focus

The majority of people suffer from this in their lives and careers. They may be mid-flow on a project and an email or phone call comes in. Their attention is distracted, they read the emails or take the call. The call may last longer than expected, or they may browse the Internet whilst doing their emails and before they know it it's mid-afternoon. They're doing lots of tasks at once, but really nothing is actually getting done.

I have been there and let me tell you it is not productive.

When you try to grab too much then you often don't grab anything at all. I often see it happen, someone trying the latest 'get rich quick' scheme, or trying the latest strategy that has diverted their attention. Either that or someone hears about a new area that is going to boom, and so they buy all over the place which is not a good idea for many different reasons mentioned earlier.

It is all lack of focus and clarity. The more you spread yourself, the fewer steps forward you often take. This can be hard because as mentioned earlier there are so many different strategies available in property, and there are always newer more 'niched' strategies coming to market. Whilst these may seem appealing and turn your head initially, it is vital that you focus on your own strategy and plan, and work on the most important things for you at that point. Only once you have achieved your initial goal and mastered one strategy should you move on.

5. Not having a cash buffer

The investors who get into trouble are often the ones who do not have access to spare cash in case of an emergency. As an investor you can incur unexpected costs and so you must have some spare cash to cover these times. The size of this buffer depends on your personal level of risk.

6. Putting all your eggs in one basket

We covered the importance of not relying on one income stream earlier in the book, and it is definitely something to avoid. This does also apply to putting all your eggs in one basket with things other than just income streams. It also applies to covering all bases of your property business. For example it is important to not just rely on one refurbishment team or mortgage broker, in case they are unavailable in times of need. If you are sourcing properties for others then always keeping a back-up buyer in case anything happens is key, and minimises your risk of the property purchase falling through. Whatever the situation is make sure you have a plan B and are not exposed.

7. Ignoring properties that are sold subject to contract (SSTC)

If you ignore properties that are SSTC, then there is a good chance that you will be leaving lots of potentially good deals on the table. Many deals are done after a property has been under offer for a variety of reasons. Firstly once an offer has been accepted the buyer may find out that they cannot get the finance that they require. Now I always suggest that people get a mortgage approved before putting in an offer if they can, but some people do not do this and then find out that they cannot get a mortgage, therefore the sale cannot proceed. Secondly, sometimes when a survey is done on a property when it has sold, if there are faults then this is when they will be revealed. When properties come to market a lot of the time no one spots potential faults because the average person, including some agents, don't know what to look for. There is often a lot of emotion, and if they like the property and are going to live in it, they are mainly focusing on the cosmetic aspect of the property. If faults do get highlighted during survey then many times people will pull out of the sale and not proceed. You want to make sure that you track the sale if you are interested in a particular property, to make sure that if it does fall through you get the first call.

8. Not gathering relevant information and not following up

Gathering relevant information seems so obvious but it is not always collected by people. You need relevant information and it needs to be current. I often see time wasted getting the wrong information, which is not productive. You want as much information as possible but getting the seller's name, an up to date landline and mobile number and email is the absolute least you want. This is needed for the next stage of following up. Remember earlier I talked about 'sold subject to contract' properties, and having a follow up system. Your offer may not be accepted straight away, or the vendor might not even be ready to sell at that point so following up regularly to see if things have changed is key. By not following up you are potentially leaving many profitable properties on the table.

It is so important you avoid these mistakes to allow yourself the best chance of success.

Summary: These are common mistakes that I have seen occur over the last eight years. Avoid these at all costs and you will be successful. Fall foul of them and they can really harm your chances of success.

SO WHAT CAN YOU DO NOW?

Firstly, I sincerely hope that you have enjoyed reading this book and have learnt a great deal from it. When I sat down to write this book my objective was to share with you the incredible knowledge I have gained over the last eight years I have been in property. I was fortunate enough to have some great mentors in that time who opened the doors for me to a wealth of knowledge that really changed my life.

The other objective of the book was to inspire and motivate others to realise that you can do the same if you learn the information and have the right guidance and support along the way. I hope this book has also highlighted the fact that there are multiple strategies available in property, and the key is finding out which one is right for you and can help you achieve your goals.

This book has been based more on the core fundamentals of property investing and the attitudes and beliefs that I have found many successful investors to have. These are key and are a fantastic base to start your journey successfully. There are however ways to take your knowledge to the next level, and below are things you can do now if you want to progress further:

1. Email me

Yes you heard it right, you can email me directly and you will not get an automated response or a member of my team. I pride myself on speaking with people directly by email or phone and will be more than happy to discuss with you your current situation, and your goals moving forward. My email is peter@embraceproperty.com and I would be happy to hear from you.

2. My Group Mentoring programme

I personally offer a tailored mentoring programme which is designed to help individuals who are looking to further their property education and career. This programme is a yearly programme which is designed to provide full accountability and support throughout the year. You will be given monthly access to not just me but also be able to access my power team and network of contacts should you wish to. For more information you can also email me.

3. Embrace Property events

At Embrace Property we provide a variety of events to support people on their journey into property. These range from our introductory seminars and networking events, right through to our one day courses on a range of different topics. These events will highlight the different strategies available to you, such as the HMO strategy and the deal packaging strategy, to name just a couple.

For information on these please visit www.embraceproperty.com/events to find out more.

BONUS CHAPTER: WHAT WOULD I DO IF I WAS STARTING OUT AGAIN TODAY?

I am often asked nowadays what I would do if I was to start out today. It is a topic of conversation that occurs regularly and something I think about fairly frequently myself. This is because the market has changed since I started out in property. Now I feel that it is important to stress here that I am writing this with the benefit of knowing what I know now rather than coming from a cold start in terms of knowledge. This is why I feel I am well placed to give my opinion on what I would do, and hope these experiences I have had will help new people starting out who are reading this.

There has been lots of change in the economy and property world since I started in 2007 and some of the strategies that were working then may not necessarily be working now and vice versa.

What I truly believe always remains constant are the core fundamentals which I have explained in this book. There is certainly no substitute for learning the basic fundamentals of property investing and this is something that I constantly suggest my mentees do when they are starting out. With the amount of creative strategies out there today, and the fancy eye-catching strategies, it can be very appealing to look into these first and take your eye off the core fundamentals.

These are the fundamentals of finding a goldmine area, planning your strategy and goals, learning the basics of property investment, to name just a few. I quickly learnt in property investing that without a goldmine area and the ability to find and finance properties, then the other things just do not work. If you can't find the right properties then you can have all the strategies in the world, the harsh reality is that they won't work.

So with his in mind the first thing I would do if I was starting out today would be to plan my strategy and then begin to look for an area that would accommodate this. I always recommend that someone starting out with little property investment knowledge should start out buying a couple of single let properties first that do not need huge refurbishments to get them to a rentable standard. Then after this if they decide to, they are better placed in my opinion to move onto bigger projects such as an HMO property that may need a bigger refurbishment, and other compliance such as a licence. This is because I believe that by doing this you can learn from smaller projects first, and then move on once you have gained the confidence and knowledge to do so. Property investing is a big step for many people and it can take time to get used to being a landlord and having multiple properties. This is not necessarily a bad thing, and it is always better to ease yourself in when you start. This is exactly what I did when I started and I found it to be a good leveller and something that allowed me to progress at the right speed. Unfortunately this was not always the case with other people, and some people I knew took on huge projects initially and just didn't have the contacts, knowledge or experience to undertake these projects. Unfortunately in many cases they lost time and money and I would hate that to be the case with you.

As a general rule my biggest aim is to create the largest cash flow from an asset, by also leaving the smallest amount of money possible in a property purchase, to maximise my return on investment. An example of this would be a property I purchased recently. The property I purchased cost £80,000 and cost £7,000 to refurbish to the required rentable standard. Therefore with the 25% deposit, the £7,000 refurbishment cost, and the other buying fees, the total was just shy of £30,000. This particular property gives me a net income of £7,000 per year after all costs and so based on this it provides a return on investment of 23% (£7,000/ £30,000). Now this is before re-financing the property and taking any money back out of the property. Once I do this, then the return on investment increases significantly and infinitely.

The beauty of starting out with your strategy and plan is that it is then possible to test and measure this, and make your decisions based on solid figures and not theory. I have found this to be vitally important and it takes a period of time, usually at least 6 months, to get a good solid set of numbers to analyse that strategy and how the investment is doing. This is key as you want to test and tweak your strategy before buying lots of units like this, again to minimise risk which we spoke about earlier on.

I have found this to be paramount during my time in property and by doing this it has uncovered different things, often very subtle, that have made huge differences. For example, when I was initially finding my investment area I realised that one area did not always work for both an HMO and single let strategy. I also found that when undertaking HMOs, going that step further in terms of refurbishment meant that I was able to attract higher rents, and the tenants were happy to stay longer term. This made the profitability of the asset higher which was highlighted by testing this over time.

So back to what I would do if I was starting out today, and it would be a mix of the above. From my years in property, I have seen people usually fall into one of two categories: those who have money to invest currently, and those who are looking for finance or strategies that do not require as much start-up capital.

If I was starting out today with no cash currently available, I would still begin to scan my local area or within 20-30 miles if possible, and start looking for properties that could fit my strategy for single lets, which in this case would be at least an 8-10% yield and at least £200 per month net cash flow. Then you would have multiple options which often people feel you do not have if you have no money available. You would be able to sell the properties onto other investors and charge a fee which as mentioned in chapter nine is a fantastic strategy. You would also be able to look at joint venturing with others which again was mentioned in chapter nine. As you can see there are always options and ways to move forward, if you think creatively.

Now these sorts of terms and ways of thinking used to be unfamiliar and daunting to me. But I got educated, learned very quickly and they became second nature. So I know you can do the same too.

It would be at this point (as I did at the start) that I would look to surround myself with likeminded people, and the importance of this cannot be stressed enough. It is why I felt it had to be a chapter in its own right earlier in the book. Now this can be done in a variety of ways but starting at your own local property networking event is a great start. If you type 'property networking' into an internet search tool and then your town you will likely find quite a few. These events are a great way to meet people and start to learn more about property investing in general.

You will be investing in yourself from a time standpoint here, and it is then up to you whether you decide to take this a step further and invest financially in your property education. Now this can often be something that people starting out are very sceptical of. This is because there are many property education firms or individuals out there, and as with all walks of life there will be some who are not ethical and just there to take as much money from people as they can. There are on the other hand also many other firms (and I like to think the majority are ethical) who are there to support you on your property journey to help you to achieve your goals. You will need to find the one that sits right with you, but I have found that investing in my education has been vitally important and given me a huge return. I recommend this highly to people as one of the best investments they can make, but finding the right people for you is key.

As a conclusion and to sum up, no one size fits all. It is important to follow the points mentioned in this book and to do your research. You do have to remember though that your individual circumstances may not be the same as someone else's, so you will need to look at what help and support you need as an individual to reach your goals.

I truly hope you are able to get all the success you desire, and that I see you around the property circuit one day talking about your journey and results.

To your success
Best wishes
Peter Iwaniszewski

Bonus: Download your free report 'Ten top tips a beginner can use to start their property journey today' and your free 30 minute consultation.

The report will give you more information and further tips on what to look out for when investing in property. It will identify simple steps that even a beginner can make to start investing in property today. You can download it here www.embraceproperty.com

The consultation will be focused around you and your investment goals. I will be able to sit down with you, or discuss over the phone, your current situation and where you would like property investment to take you in the future. I will be able to give you the benefit of my experience, and give you my opinion on what strategies I think would be best for you to start out with, based on your own individual circumstances. Every person's circumstances is different, and so I will take the time to find out what is important to you long term, which will give you the best chance of success. You can call the office on 02476158187 to book in a suitable time.

Case Study from Phil and Lorraine Thompson.

"Phil had been playing with property on and off for about 12 years but had never really taken the bull by the horns. We were on holiday and Phil had taken a couple of books to read, after reading one of them he said, "there is a young guy in this book that is an inspiration I'm going to contact him." Phil met up with Peter and over coffee they agreed to meet again with myself in tow, which was a turning point for me as I felt that Peter was so grounded and knowledgeable and sincere. The day we started in mentorship with Peter really started us on our property journey and within 6 months we had 2 properties. Having monthly meetings with Pete where we would be accountable was what we needed, it worked so well that before the year was up we had sourced 2 more properties. We have gone from strength to strength with Pete's help and advice. So if you are starting out on your property journey, you should really consider Pete's mentorship programme, he will hold your hand as much as you want him to."

Case study from Chris Pagett:

"I started Peter's mentorship course at Embrace in January 2015. Before I started the mentorship I was going from different courses trying to find my property investing strategy. I had some understanding of deal packaging and tried to build a business from this and make some cash flow to invest in property but I found I was not getting any deals. I found Peter after listening to a JV audio set in my car and found his success story very interesting as he was a young investor I felt he could help and support me. I first attended a day course and really found the day helpful. I then met Peter at his office and told him about my goals and passion for property, and the need for support with my business. On that day I signed up for the mentorship. I have now been with Peter at Embrace for 8 months and found my first two rent to rent properties that cash flow £1,200 per month and Peter supported me to set them up and manage them. I would say to anyone in property you need support if you want to make a success out of property."

A BIG THANK YOU

Thanks to all those who have supported me along the way, family and friends, you know who you are. I would like to thank my mum dad and all my family who have been a great support over my life and in my business. I may not say it enough but all your help and support is appreciated and always noticed.

Thanks to Aimee and Lauren at Embrace for all your hard work and helping with the cover design of the book.

Thanks to Stephanie Hale at Oxford Literary Consultancy for support and guidance while writing this book.

Also thank you to Jackie Goodman for proof reading the book and spotting any spelling mistakes that were in there. Hopefully there were not too many ☺

I would also like to thank all of those who said I couldn't succeed and that it was the wrong time to invest in property. You inspired me more than you will ever know to take action and change my life.

And finally I would also like to thank you if you are reading this now. You are in the 5% and you will succeed as long as you follow your dreams and do not listen to negative opinions out there. Thank you sincerely for reading this book.

#0053 - 180416 - C0 - 210/148/14 - PB - DID1427551